'Gone With The Wind' In Madagascar

'GONE WITH THE WIND' IN MADAGASCAR

▼

A Cruise To An Indian Ocean Paradise

Avril Sellars

Writers Club Press

San Jose New York Lincoln Shanghai

'Gone With The Wind' In Madagascar
A Cruise To An Indian Ocean Paradise

Writers Club Press
an imprint of iUniverse.com, Inc.

For information address:
iUniverse.com, Inc.
5220 S 16th, Ste. 200
Lincoln, NE 68512
www.iuniverse.com

ISBN: 0-595-19262-9

Printed in the United States of America

For cruising sailors everywhere. May you always have an inch of water under your keel . . .

CONTENTS

LIST OF ILLUSTRATIONS

FRONT COVER: Nosy Komba. The beach at Ampangorinana.
MAP OF MADAGASCAR.
'Gone With The Wind', Morganocean 31 on which Avril and Don made their voyage.

Majunga. The anchorage by the Pointe de Sable.

Majunga. Typical pirogues return to Bombetoka Bay after a day's fishing.

Majunga. Our dinghy 'gardien' Dex at the Port aux Boutres (small craft harbour).

Majunga. Don tries an unusual mode of transport, a 'pousse-pousse'.

Majunga. Baobab tree on the beachfront, reputed to be 700 years old.

Nosy Iranja. At low tide, Avril explores the sandspit joining the two exquisite islands.

Nosy Iranja. On the sandspit, looking towards the smaller island. Beyond is Madagascar.

Nosy Komba. Don and friends at the Lemur Park at Ampangorinana.

Nosy Komba. Enjoying a beer in paradise.....

Nosy Komba....and here comes the ice!

Nosy Komba. The beach at Ampangorinana, looking south east to the mountains of Madagascar.

Nosy Mitsio. The one that didn't get away. Don and the wahoo he bagged with a piece of silver paper as bait!

Nosy Mitsio. Don explores the hills above Maribe Bay. Nosy Be and the basalt rocks known as Les Quatres Frères are in the background.

Nosy Mitsio. 'Gone With The Wind' rides peacefully at anchor as the sun sets over Nosy Ankarea.

BACK COVER: Avril and Don Sellars, safely back in Durban after their trip.

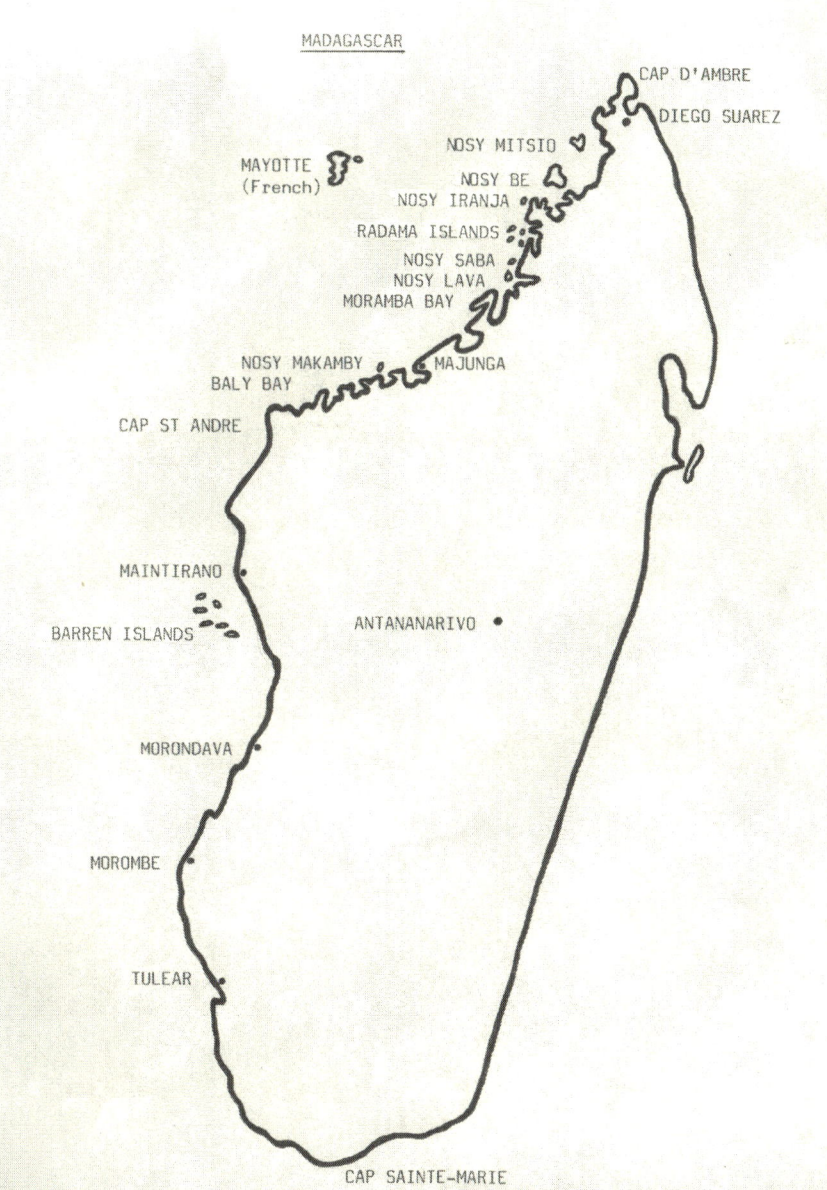

MADAGASCAR

CAP D'AMBRE

DIEGO SUAREZ

NOSY MITSIO

MAYOTTE
(French)

NOSY BE
NOSY IRANJA
RADAMA ISLANDS
NOSY SABA
NOSY LAVA
MORAMBA BAY

NOSY MAKAMBY   MAJUNGA
BALY BAY

CAP ST ANDRE

MAINTIRANO

ANTANANARIVO

BARREN ISLANDS

MORONDAVA

MOROMBE

TULEAR

CAP SAINTE-MARIE

INTRODUCTION

This is the really boring part, so please feel free to skip it and move on to the main body of the text. To tell you the truth, I wouldn't be writing this at all if my publisher hadn't been the conscientious type who believes the reader should get his money's worth and sets a minimum verbiage limit of 30000 words on each 'oeuvre'. Well, be that as it may, I thought perhaps I should use it as an opportunity to give you some background on myself and Don and how we got into sailing and how we got to where we are today. Not that I subscribe much to the theory that you can learn from other people's experiences. I believe everyone has to try things for him or herself and learn by his or her mistakes. It may be painful, but in the end it is the best teacher. However, for those of you still hooked on reading about other people's lives, in fact for those of you still *reading*, here goes....

Well, it all started, I suppose, with our growing dissatisfaction with our life in Scotland. It was the early 1980s. The era of a rampant Margaret Thatcher, bloodthirsty Falklands War jingoism and a shrivelling up of Scotland's will to freedom following the disastrous 1979 General Election results for the Scottish National Party. At that time something like 98% of school-leavers in our county were unemployed, with little prospect of finding any work except through short-term government schemes.

Unemployment generally was rising, and many firms were going to the wall. With both of us in secure employment, Don and I were the fortunate ones in this bleak landscape.

The bitter, final blow for us was the sudden death of Don's father in 1981. Our anchor was gone. He was not only a beloved father, but a mentor and work colleague for Don in his dental practice, and his unquenchable enthusiasm and love of life had drawn everybody to him. A malaise settled on us. There seemed little purpose in carrying on. Life would never be quite the same again. So we started making enquiries about emigrating. At that time it seemed that only 'pariah' countries such as Libya and South Africa still had their doors wide open to professional people. Both countries were sorely in need of a good PR job. Fortunately for us, we decided to give Libya a miss and I had relatives in South Africa and knew a little bit about the country, so South Africa it was. It so happened that Don had taken on a dental associate around this time, who expressed an interest in buying the practice and living quarters from us. It was all beginning to fall into place.

Don got a job with a practice near Durban, on the east coast, and flew out in January 1983. I was left behind to 'finalize' the packing and shipping of our effects. Although the removals people were marvellous, I still found myself waking in a cold sweat in the early hours of each morning, my brain racing with all the tasks still to be done in the ever-shrinking time available. In life, what doesn't kill us makes us stronger, as they say, so I guess this was just the first of several strengthening lessons for me along life's path. I was certainly glad when the removals were all over and I could step aboard that plane to South Africa in the March of that year. Of course, there were tearful farewells to family and friends, but overall we felt it was a positive move and one we had to make at that time or regret for the rest of our lives.

Africa! It was love at first sight for me. The sounds, the smells, the colours, the dazzling light all burst upon my jaded European senses. It was a big land with a big heart. I felt like a pot-bound plant suddenly transplanted into a rich and limitless soil, in which I was free to spread my roots and grow as I pleased. For Don too, the complete change of lifestyle and working environment was a revelation. And the political situation? Well, having grown up with the anti-apartheid line put forward by much of the British media, we were prepared to believe *anything* about South Africa. I have to say that when we got there we were very pleasantly surprised. Of course as Europeans we found ourselves part of an elite in a country where, as it was said, any dumb cluck could make a go of it provided he had a white skin! But that was only a small part of the whole story. The wisest comment I ever heard about South Africa was by the British writer and broadcaster, Malcolm Muggeridge. He said you could make two diametrically opposed films about South Africa, and they would both be equally true. I think that gives an inkling of the enormous complexities and paradoxes of the South African political situation.

As for getting ourselves established there, it was by no means all plain sailing. After a year Don decided to set up his own practice from scratch in one of the suburbs of Durban and we worked very hard to get the new business off the ground. I remember our first month's meagre earnings were less than R1400 (US$200)! At the same time, I was trying to get a new home and garden established under very different climatic and social conditions from those I had been accustomed to. For one thing, I had to get used to employing African domestic staff, which can be a mixed blessing. It was great to have help with the heavy, tedious chores, but one was expected to take on a depth of responsibility for one's employees almost akin to that of a tribal chief. Whenever a bureaucratic, domestic or financial problem afflicted an employee or his or her family, the employer was looked to as the person to sort it all out. Perhaps because of this, one could sense a very real bond of respect and friendship between most employers and their staff that is difficult for people who have not lived under that system to understand.

Apartheid was a morally indefensible system, yet paradoxically its rigid framework gave a certain stability to everyday life in those days. We all knew the rules; we all knew our relative places in society, so we could relax and not worry too much about it. Besides, the province in which we were living had a long tradition of liberalism amongst the white, largely English-speaking middle classes, as well as a large, independent-minded Zulu population, so there was always just a whiff of subversion in the air. For our own part, we always tried to deal fairly and honestly with everyone we came in contact with, regardless of race. I like to think we always did the best we could as far as our employees were concerned and they repaid us richly with long years of loyal service. We were only too delighted when we found ourselves in a position to assist our domestic servant in building a house for herself and her dependants in her township. In the wider social sphere too, we were happy to be able to participate in the work of organisations such as Rotary International. The highlights of our local Rotary Club membership were Don's year as Chairman and his success in obtaining international funding for an African mission hospital project near Durban. For this, the club members awarded Don a Paul Harris Fellowship, Rotary's highest honour.

It was only after the ending of apartheid that the full story of the horrors committed in its name was revealed. The facts unearthed by the Truth and Reconciliation Commission under Desmond Tutu were truly shocking to much of the South African population, who had been kept almost totally in the dark for all those years. But at the time we emigrated to South Africa the genuine feeling, certainly amongst the white population, was that the country was being unfairly singled out for sanctions because it had made the big mistake of codifying what had in fact been happening tacitly, since time immemorial, in many countries of the world. There were also champions of the liberal cause, such as Helen Suzman, who were against sanctions on the grounds that they were hurting the very people they were supposed to be helping—the black Africans. Also, it has to be said that good and bad were by no means clear cut. One side's 'terrorists' were the other side's 'freedom fighters', but behind the labels were some appalling acts of murder and maiming of innocent civilians by means of bombs planted in or near crowded shops, bars and restaurants. It was difficult to be sympathetic to people who could use such means, no matter how just their cause.

Whatever the pros and cons of the political debate, the end effect for people living in South Africa during the 1980s was that the country tended to turn more and more in on itself. Businesses worked tirelessly on 'import substitution', including weaponry and other military hardware. Sport became a great galvanizing force and clubs proliferated. Standards of education and healthcare were second to none (at least for the whites or other races who could afford to buy them privately). The cost of living was low, and regular entertaining at home or in 'country clubs' or restaurants was the norm. Without exception, our neighbours were kind and welcoming towards us. Society was pervaded by an old-world graciousness and genuine 'good manners' that had long ago disappeared from British life. No wonder the province of Natal, where we were living, was affectionately known as 'the last outpost of the British Empire'.

This then was the backdrop to our new life in South Africa. With all the advantages of climate, opportunity, education and relative financial security, we did things we would never have believed possible in our previous existence. We joined a flying club and Don learned to fly. I joined a yacht club and took a sailing course with a local sailing academy. I can still remember, as if it were yesterday, the precise moment when the breeze freshened offshore and the yacht I was on began to heel and gather speed and I thought to myself 'yes, this is it; this is what I want to do'! Besides sailing and flying, we took part in a variety of other sports and activities. We made new friends, many of them expatriates like ourselves. In professional life too, Don found far more opportunity to develop his expertise and special interests than he would have done under the British National Health Service. We took the opportunity to travel and see some of South Africa's spectacular scenery and explore her national parks and game reserves. All in all we revelled in our marvellous new life. Migrating had given us the boot up the backside we needed to get out and do all these wonderful things.

Towards the end of 1984, my parents decided to apply for immigration into South Africa to be closer to us. They sold up their house and packed up all their belongings. Then, on 1 January 1985, my father suffered a heart attack and it looked as though their planned departure would have to be delayed. A few days later their immigration clearance came through from the South African authorities. On the evening of the same day, my father suffered a second, devastating heart attack. Sadly, he did not recover. I flew over to Scotland to be with my mother who, understandably, was in a state of shock. Her whole world had been turned upside down. Dad was dead, the house had been sold and all their belongings were in a container on a ship on its way to South Africa. After the funeral, I brought my mother out to stay with us until we were able to get her settled in a place of her own, close by us. However, she never really came to terms with the loss of my father and all the turmoil of moving to a strange new country. What a life they would have enjoyed if only Dad had survived, but it was not to be.

Another dream that was not to be was for us to start a family of our own. Then, out of the blue, in 1987 I discovered that I had breast cancer. Things happened very quickly after that. I was whisked into hospital and ended up having to undergo a mastectomy, followed by weeks of radiation therapy and months of chemotherapy. It was another of life's hard lessons.

At times the treatment left me so sick and depressed that I felt as though I were dying. It was an experience I would not wish on anyone. But with the tremendous love and support of my wonderful husband, family and friends, I did emerge from that dark place. I decided I was jolly well not going to give up and die.

So, just a few weeks after the surgery I got permission from my specialist to sail on a yacht to the island of Mauritius, in the Indian Ocean, just beyond Madagascar. The voyage was a training exercise organised by the same sailing academy that had got me all fired up about keelboat sailing in the first place. It was my first ocean passage and it was an unforgettable experience. Perhaps the best thing about it was that I was allowed to stop taking the awful chemotherapy drugs for the duration of the voyage. My specialist had also given me a supply of vitamin B12 capsules to take, so I felt on top of the world again. The psychological boost it gave me was just what I needed. I think I also began to realise then the importance of having something to look forward to, something to work towards. In some vague way, I knew that sailing was going to play a big part in my future life.

The following year Don and I bought our first keelboat. It was a 30-foot Royal Cape One Design called 'Little One', a very seaworthy if less than luxurious sloop, on which we raced and cruised out of Durban harbour, and generally practised our sailing skills. A couple of years later we had a new 'Little One' built, cannibalising several bits and pieces off the old boat. By now, Don found sailing more exciting than his flying, so he was well and truly hooked. We both acquired various sailing qualifications that would stand us in good stead in the years to come. Whenever we could, we took the opportunity to crew on other people's boats and do yacht deliveries, learning all the time from our varied experiences.

I was also getting involved in the promotion of women's sailing in South Africa. My first experience of an all-girl team was in 1989, when I joined the crew of a 34-foot sloop in a race from Mauritius to Durban. Some of my happiest memories and most enduring friendships came out of that trip. I began skippering my own all-girl teams on 'Little One' in regattas and offshore races. It was by no means an easy training ground, for the east coast of South Africa is notorious as one of the most dangerous in the world. The reason for this is the sometimes deadly combination of a strong current, (the Agulhas Current) flowing south-westwards down the coast, meeting a sudden south-westerly gale advancing up the coast against the current, resulting in the build-up of steep, freakish seas. To make matters worse, the coast provides very few safe refuges to duck into in the event of bad weather catching you out. One has to learn very quickly the arts of weather prediction and heavy weather helming on such a coast. I am proud to say that my female crews on some of those gruelling races proved to be amongst the bravest and finest it has been my privilege to sail with—and they were not all-white!

Sadly, 1989 was the year that my mother died. There had been a flu epidemic and she soon succumbed to the infection, her lungs weakened by chronic emphysema. (She never could give up smoking.) I was with her at the hospital when she slipped away. More 'might have beens' had to be put away; another inevitable, yet painful, step along life's path had to be negotiated.

On a happier note, that year also saw a visit from Don's mother, a bundle of energy, who embarked upon an exploration of the country, with particular emphasis on the study of succulent plants. After a marvellous trip we did together on the luxurious Blue Train from Johannesburg to Cape Town, she set off on her travels with a guide. She visited all kinds of habitats, from private and botanical gardens to the wild surroundings of the Richtersveld, in the far west of the country. It was wonderful to see her pursuing her lifetime passion for cacti and succulents, about which she is an authority and which, I am happy to say, she continues to this day.

By the early 1990s we were really getting into our sailing. We moved from the outer suburbs into Durban to be nearer the yacht club, around which much of our leisure time revolved. I and some women friends started up a branch of the South African Ladies' Sailing Association, 'SALSA' for short, and we got various women's sailing events off the ground. I began sailing the little J22 (22-foot) racing yachts which were popular amongst the women sailing on inland waters in the Johannesburg area. In fact, I ended up buying a fairly old one, which I brought down to Durban and which required a considerable amount of work to bring it up to racing condition. After many weeks of sanding and filling the pitted bottom, I finally got the little boat to the stage where she was ready for her final paint job. As we stood admiring her, a friend asked me what I was going to call her and suggested it should be something with a bit of spice and oomph in it! The name 'Hot Salsa!' popped into my head and that was what we called her. I and my all-girl crew sailed her for several years, eventually competing in the J22 World Championships in Cape Town in 1997. I can honestly say—and even Don will agree with me—that the time we had with the little J22 was the most fun we ever had in sailing. I was able to trailer the little boat all over the country and compete in a variety of events, meeting similarly enthusiastic people wherever I went. It was no surprise to find that the J22s formed the biggest class of racing keelboat in South Africa.

With all the activity centred on the J22, our other boat, 'Little One', tended to be rather neglected and we began to think about selling her. A long-term dream was beginning to form in our minds: to get ourselves a big comfortable boat that would be suitable for cruising. During the early 1990s we spent a couple of spells cruising with friends in the Caribbean and encountered several perfectly sane people who had managed to turn their cruising dreams into reality. So why not us? I particularly liked one cruising man's description of what his old age would be like: it's when you're snorkelling on a coral reef and you start to feel a pain in your chest and you say to yourself 'er, I think I'll just swim back to the boat now…' What a way to go!

However, we still had a way to go before our cruising life became a reality and a few more hard knocks to endure en route. In 1990 I was asked to crew on a long ocean race from Cape Town to Lisbon, Portugal. I was away for about three months altogether and found it a rather strange and disturbing experience. I was with a small, mixed crew on a large comfortable ketch and although it was interesting to visit such places as St Helena Island, the Cape Verde Islands and the Azores, the psychological tensions that built up between members of the crew made life unpleasant and at times downright frightening. It was a totally new dimension to long distance sailing, which until then I had been unaware of and about which I had to learn rapidly in order to preserve my sanity!

Not so very long after that something else happened that was to have a profound effect on our lives. It was an episode that began innocuously enough. It had become the tradition for the yacht clubs to run 'fun races' in Durban harbour every Wednesday evening during the summer months, which in the southern hemisphere means from October to March. One year it was decided that for Valentine's Day we would hold a 'ladies' race' where each boat would be helmed by a woman and women would be encouraged to participate as much as possible. I was to assist with the actual running of the race from the committee boat and Don skippered a mixed crew on 'Little One', with a talented young female dinghy-sailor on the helm. There was a big turnout of yachts, virtually all of which had plenty of ladies on their crews and a lady on the helm. However, I noticed one sloop which we had not seen out racing for quite some time, with no women on board and being helmed by her owner. We assumed he had not read the sailing instructions about it being a 'ladies' race' and thought no more about it.

The race started without incident, but then, about halfway through, we heard an agitated radio message from one of the rescue boats out on the course. 'Little One' had been involved in a collision with the 'all-male' sloop and one of her crew was gravely injured. I couldn't believe it. Surely there was some mistake. This was just a 'fun race' after all! Aboard the committee boat we decided to let the race continue, to enable the casualty to be got ashore without panic. At this stage, I did not know who it was who had been hurt, but it sounded bad. The 'all-male' sloop passed us on her way back to the marina and then came 'Little One'. I was relieved to see Don on the helm. At least he was all right. I wanted to get to him as quickly as possible, but we still had a whole race to finish. By the time I got ashore, the ambulance had picked up the casualty and left. Don was in a terrible state and I could see that 'Little One' had been badly damaged. I finally learned the devastating news that it was one of the women on board who had been hurt, a good friend and stalwart crew of mine. She was fortunate to have survived the accident, but she lost a foot and because of that the course of her life was utterly changed.

In the immediate aftermath, Don and I withdrew from the company of other people. It had hit us as severely as a bereavement. But that was when true friends rallied round and helped in so many ways: cleaning up the boat, taking photos of the damage, etc. The victim herself was incredibly brave and, in fact, at our first meeting with her in the hospital, she was the one who had us all laughing and chatting away like a big family reunion. We didn't know it then, but after the initial shock had abated, the whole affair was to drag on over the course of several years, becoming the subject of enquiries, a court case and seemingly endless deliberations.

The facts of the case were that 'Little One' had been sailing downwind in a shipping channel towards the next turning mark, on starboard tack (i.e. she had right of way over yachts on the port tack). Several yachts, including the one that collided with her, were approaching, beating on port tack, having already rounded the turning mark. The crew of 'Little One' were keeping a lookout and became concerned when they perceived that a risk of collision existed with that one particular yacht. As they came closer, 'Little One' judged that the other yacht was not taking the required action to avoid collision, so she altered course to leeward of the other yacht and towards the edge of the channel. At this stage the two yachts would have passed each other safely, if they had both remained on their courses. However, the other yacht suddenly altered course towards 'Little One' and hit her amidships, at speed and at right-angles, in the type of collision known as a T-bone. The crew-member who was injured had been standing on the deck of 'Little One', by the shrouds, when she saw the imminent risk of collision. She shouted a warning, saw the head of a crew-man appear around a sail on the other yacht and tried to scramble backwards towards the cockpit. The bow of the other yacht hit 'Little One' with such force that it rode right up over the coachroof and deck on the starboard side. The victim's foot was crushed and virtually sliced off on top of the coachroof, and not hanging over the side of the deck, as many misleading stories tried to make out. In addition, the force of the impact threw the victim down the companionway stairs into the cabin below, breaking some of her ribs. Damage to 'Little One' included holes torn in the coachroof and side deck, metal and wooden fittings sliced through, loosened keel bolts, broken shrouds and a mast so badly twisted it had to be replaced.

The insurance company were marvellous and settled immediate medical bills and repairs to the boat, but there were insufficient funds to cover everything, particularly the question of compensation. This led to a civil court case being brought against both yachts, which was to hang over us and blight our lives for such a long time. Eventually, 'Little One' and Don, as the skipper, were completely exonerated. The owner/skipper of the other yacht was held entirely to blame for the collision and no doubt paid dearly, losing his yacht into the bargain. For us, it was like a heavy weight being lifted off our shoulders. We had learned some painful and costly lessons along the way. As for our injured friend, she learned to walk with her artificial leg, drove a specially adapted car and went sailing again, this time on a cruising boat in the Mediterranean, where she met a charming cruising yachtsman and sailed away with him.

Obviously, such traumatic experiences leave their mark. 'Little One' was expertly repaired and we did continue to sail her, but we were now looking seriously at selling her. The sale went through and I turned my attention to preparations for the J22 World Championships in Cape Town. While all this was going on, a young couple arrived in Durban on an eye-catching 31-foot yacht in which they had just completed a six-year long circumnavigation of the world. The yacht was a Morganocean 31 called 'Gone With The Wind'.

Strange how fate takes a hand. We had not planned to get a cruising boat quite so soon, but when we discovered 'Gone With The Wind' was for sale we had to see her and as soon as we stepped aboard her we had to have her! She was in such immaculate condition that she passed her survey with flying colours. As a friend of ours said at the time, always go for a 'poor man's boat' rather than a rich man's toy, because you know it will have been well looked after. He wasn't wrong. We bought 'Gone With The Wind' towards the end of 1996 and have been very happy with her ever since. The name was not our choice, but we rather liked it and decided to keep it. Besides, all old salts will tell you it's very bad luck to change the name of a vessel!

After the J22 Worlds I sold 'Hot Salsa!', and soon we had disposed of our house and much of our worldly goods in order to live aboard 'Gone With The Wind'. It was quite an undertaking, but, as with our emigration all those years before, it was something we were ready for and it was a strangely liberating experience. The boat wasn't exactly spacious, but we settled in and it soon became 'home' to us, although as soon as friends knew we were living on the boat, they inundated us with offers for us to 'house sit' for them! We had a marvellous and varied year or two doing that, while Don wound up the dental practice.

Then, out of the blue, another friend asked us to help him take his yacht from Annapolis, Maryland, across the Atlantic to the British Isles. That was in 1999. We spent about 7 months on our friend's boat and had a fascinating time sailing her from Annapolis down to Norfolk, Virginia, and from there to Bermuda and the Azores, finishing up in Ireland and finally the west coast of Scotland. It was the first long ocean crossing that Don and I had done together and it was a great learning experience for both of us. Above all, it enabled us to see at first hand all the joys and pitfalls of cruising.

Our venture in 1999 across the Atlantic had sidetracked us somewhat from our own timetable of starting our cruising life aboard 'Gone With The Wind' that year. We had to wait until the following year to get going. The momentous year 2000 saw us finally embarking upon our long dreamed of cruise to Madagascar, Mayotte and the eastern coast of Africa. The account of much of that trip can be found in the following chapters. We hope you will find it as entertaining to read about as we did to actually live it.

When I look back on all that has happened in my life, I can't help thinking how lucky I have been. Although not every experience has been a pleasant one, the sum total of all the events and the amazing people in my life have shaped me and brought me to where I am today. Above all, I am glad I had a great dream and have been able to live that dream. But I'm nothing special. Anyone can do it. If you want it badly enough you will find a way to make your dream come true. It's frightening to take the first step into the unknown, wondering whether you are making a big mistake and whether you are going to make a fool of yourself. But if we never made mistakes we wouldn't learn anything. So, don't be afraid to try new things. Always remember: the Titanic was built by professionals, Noah's Ark by amateurs!

'Gone With The Wind' In Madagascar

▼

Durban To Morombe

We finally began our long-projected Indian Ocean cruise on 15 June, 2000, leaving Durban, South Africa late in the evening by the light of a glorious full moon. The north-easter was rapidly dying and, having kept an eye on the synoptic weather charts for several days, we were hopeful of a south-wester coming through to take its place and help us on our way. Our Morganocean 31, 'Gone With The Wind', was in her element again after several years of relative inactivity sitting at Durban Marina. After being sidetracked ourselves for a year or so with such things as a yacht delivery with a friend across the Atlantic, we were also ready for the adventure that lay ahead. This was to be *our* adventure, mine and Don's, not shared with anyone else.

'Gone With The Wind' is a well-found and eminently suitable craft for such a venture. Designed and built in South Africa in 1990, she completed a circumnavigation with her first owner during the following six years, returning to Durban in 1996, where we fell in love with her and bought her. For much of the time since then, we have lived aboard her. Although only 31 feet long, she is relatively roomy and has a full keel with a capacious bilge, so that we never have water sloshing around our feet. Her hull is built of fibreglass, she is sloop-rigged with an inner forestay on which to fly a staysail and, when the wind lets us down, there is a fine, reliable 24hp inboard diesel engine.

Accommodation below decks has been nicely set up for two people. Up forward is our double berth, with plenty of storage space underneath and neat lockers all around. Aft of that is the head and wash-basin on the port side and a hanging locker to starboard. Then comes the saloon, with a table and horseshoe settee to port and a small settee to starboard. Again, the saloon is well-endowed with lockers, as well as a natty little bookshelf up behind the starboard settee. Next comes the galley, a U-shaped affair on the port side, with a gas stove, double sink, top-loading fridge and plenty of lockers.

Opposite, on the starboard side, is what one might call 'the navigation station', with a good-sized chart table, radio equipment, radar, GPS navigation system, electrical switchboard and engine ignition. Aft of the chart table is a snug quarter berth, which is used alternately by Don and myself when we are sailing, for there is always one of us on watch in the cockpit while the other grabs a few hours' sleep below. The engine is situated behind the companionway and under the cockpit, and fuel and water tanks are located either in or close to the keel. All in all, 'Gone With The Wind' is a good, seaworthy little craft.

That first night, striking out into the Agulhas Current with a light land breeze filling our sails and friendly dolphins playing all around us, we were filled with excitement, anticipation and a little apprehension. It was our first ocean crossing with 'Gone With The Wind', and this in an ocean which above all others commands respect. We had done as much as we could to prepare our boat for the voyage. Now it was up to her: 'The boat will go on looking after you long after you've given up looking after her' as an old sailing friend used to say.

'Gone With The Wind' did not let us down and, after an uneventful nine and a half-day voyage across some 800 miles of Mozambique Channel, we arrived safely at Morombe on the south-west coast of Madagascar. We had mainly light to moderate south-easterly winds for much of the way, except during the last two days when they increased to 20-30 knots as a result of a cold front advancing up the South African coast. Life on board became very uncomfortable at that time, but our doughty little vessel took the steep-faced, foamy-crested waves in her stride, under the indefatigable hand of 'Fred', our trusty self-steering device. The little discomfort we experienced was more than made up for by the many glorious days of soaking up the sun, pitting our celestial navigation skills against those of the GPS (Global Positioning System navigation device), chatting to friends on the radio, salt water 'bathies' in the cockpit and baking bread; and the glorious nights when the vast arch of the Milky Way found an echo below in the myriad sparks of phosphorescence thrown up in our wake in the warm waters of the Mozambique Channel, when we watched stars fall and the great golden moon rise out of the sea, casting its pale glow on the waves and the dancing dolphins around us. Sometimes you can even hear the dolphins sing to each other, their high-pitched notes reverberating through the hull. It is quite magical.

Regular radio contact with other yachts revealed that a gentleman called Richard and his yacht 'Chant de Mer' were already in Madagascar, at the south-western port of Tulear. When we asked about the sort of charges we could expect to pay if we cleared in there, we were dismayed to hear that South African boats were being asked for something of the order of US$50 per boat and US$18 per person for a so-called 'cruising' permit, which we had been assured was entirely unnecessary according to maritime law. Needless to say, Richard was moving on elsewhere—to Morombe, in fact, where people are friendly and things are considerably more relaxed. This knowledge, together with favourable winds, prompted us to head for Morombe too.

Morombe is a small and fairly remote town on the south-west coast, about a hundred sea miles north of Tulear. It is protected by reefs, islands and shoaling patches. We arrived off it in the early afternoon of 25 June and threaded our way between the reefs, following the leading marks on shore and leaving the channel markers to port and starboard of us. Safely through the reefs, we made our way towards a large white-hulled ketch anchored in solitary splendour just off the sandy beach. It was 'Chant de Mer' all right, but no sign of life on board. We did not want to anchor too close to him so we motored off behind him a little way and came up head to wind—at least we tried to come up to the wind, for, before we knew what was happening, we were suddenly aground on a shoal some distance out from the beach! 'Gone With The Wind' had well and truly embraced Madagascar.

The sea breeze had freshened and was threatening to push us further onto the sand, so we hastily pumped up the rubber dinghy on deck and launched it. With the aid of our little 2hp outboard engine, Don motored the dinghy into deeper water and dropped a kedge anchor to prevent us from drifting further onto the shoal. About that time, Richard putted up in his rubber dinghy, accompanied by three charming Malagasy girls. Yes, we had come in too close when trying to anchor. Richard informed us that low tide would be in about an hour's time, so we would just have to wait until the water started rising again before we could get off. He also told us he had spoken to the local Commissariat de Police and our clearance paperwork would all be taken care of the day after tomorrow (for tomorrow was the Independence Day holiday). We were grateful to him for that.

Off he putted, with the three girls, to his boat, but stood by on VHF radio in case we required any help. Apart from putting out a second anchor, there was really nothing more to be done, except wait philosophically for the tide to come in. Thankfully, the boat did not heel over too far and we were able to make ourselves a bite to eat and relax for a bit. Before long, the water had risen enough to get us floating and we cranked away on the anchor warps to pull us off. We managed to raise one anchor, but had to leave the other, which we marked with a plastic buoy for retrieval later.

By around 8pm we were safely anchored, well away from the shoaling patch and from Richard's boat. We found, as Richard had warned us, that the incoming tide produced a strong south-flowing current against the fresh south-easterly wind so that, instead of lying to the wind, our boat lay with her head towards the tidal stream. We kept an anchor watch that night, but all was well and 'Gone With The Wind' remained secure in her first Malagasy anchorage. After all the excitement and strenuous activity, we slept like the dead, rocked gently by the warm winds and waters of this peaceful place.

Next day was spent tidying the boat and ourselves after our voyage. We had a visit from Richard and later we putted across to visit him. He was an old Madagascar hand, having sailed there several times in his self-built fibreglass ketch, based on a 36-foot Bruce Roberts design. Although living in South Africa, Richard was French-born and so he had little difficulty in communicating with the 'Malgache' or Malagasy people, many of whom speak at least a little French. It was pleasant sitting aboard 'Chant de Mer', chatting and joking about our rather abrupt arrival on Malagasy 'soil' and looking across to our boat from time to time. It was still blowing fairly strongly from the south-east and, as we looked, it dawned on us that our boat was drifting further away from us. She was dragging her anchor! Fortunately, Richard had been telling us all about anchoring using two anchors in tandem on the same chain so that if one anchor was displaced the other would still hold. He had obviously had a lot of experience in conditions such as these with strong winds and tidal streams. We hopped into the rubber dinghy and chased after 'Gone With The Wind', which by now was a considerable distance away. We adopted Richard's twin anchor trick, approaching somewhat closer to the beach, and, sure enough, it worked. Despite being tossed around in the fresh breeze and the various tidal streams, our anchors remained as solid as a rock.

In all this excitement another day slipped away before we knew it and we missed the Independence Day celebrations which Richard assured us had been great fun, with music, dancing and bare-knuckle prize-fighting, which the Malgache really enjoy. We finally went ashore on the following day to present ourselves to the various authorities and deal with what the French refer to as 'paperasse'—the general bureaucratic bumf one encounters in such places. First stop was the Port Captain's office. We were greeted by a diminutive and charming gentleman with an engaging, gap-toothed smile, and his equally charming staff. Little did we know that we were entering into a tortuous and surreal twilight zone that Graham Greene or Joseph Conrad would have appreciated enormously.

We were informed that we would have to pay port dues of the order of 160000 Malagasy Francs, which sounded alarming until we worked out that it was only about R160 (US$23)! Payment of these dues would cover us for three months of cruising the Madagascar coast and calling in at any other port. This sounded suspiciously like the infamous 'cruising permit' and we objected strongly, showing the Port Captain the letter which the Malagasy Consul in Durban had given us to counteract any such demands. However, the Captain was armed with an official document of his own which stated that vessels such as ours, classified as 'navires de plaisance' (pleasure craft) had to pay port dues according to a set tariff. I argued that we were just a small yacht and not a 'navire', which is also the French word for a 'ship'. Try as we might, we could see that eventually we were going to have to accept the charges. However, we would have to get to a bank to get some money changed first. The Port Captain said he would accompany us and on the way we would call in at Customs and Immigration.

So the three of us trooped out of his spartan but neatly-painted office, and made our way down the dusty sand road beneath the welcome shade of rows of large trees. We must have made a strange sight—the Port Captain with two white-skinned 'vazahas' (foreigners), greeting all and sundry as we wended our way towards the centre of this one-horse town. Customs came first, a fairly shabby brick bungalow with a verandah and one large office wherein a rather dapper fellow presided over a few meagre racks filled with dusty papers that looked as though they dated back to the time of Napoleon, plus some disreputable sticks of furniture. Much shuffling and rubber-stamping of papers took place before we got to the real business. Monsieur le Douanier got out his electronic calculator and presented us with another figure which we were expected to pay. When we protested that we had already obtained our visas in Durban, we were told that the charge was not for us but for the boat and, surprise surprise, would cover us for every other place that we would be visiting in Madagascar. Again, it all seemed rather alarming until we figured out that all he wanted was about R30 (US$4)! Well, that was fine, but we still had to get to the bank.

Next on our route was Immigration, situated in the building of the local Commissariat de Police. This was an even more disreputable-looking building, as bare, open and dusty as a barn, frequented by skinny and slightly sinister-looking individuals who turned out to be the police. Quite well-dressed in civilian clothes and very polite, they nevertheless gave off an aura that would not have been out of place in Haïti's Tonton Macoute! One of these gentlemen perused our passports very earnestly for a while and after an exchange with our Port Captain, informed us that the person responsible for Immigration was not available at present and we would have to come back in the afternoon. Well all right. At least they had not demanded any money from us!

Back we trekked to the boat, taking our leave of the Port Captain and agreeing to meet that afternoon to complete the formalities. At the appointed hour we presented ourselves once more at his office and the three of us set out 'en promenade' for the general entertainment of the populace. This time the Port Captain had donned a smart sports jacket to complement his light trousers and natty flip-flop sandals (actually the most practical footwear on the dusty roads). He carried the full dignity of his office with aplomb. We felt scruffy in comparison, particularly after a rather wet ride ashore in the dinghy. Back to Immigration we went and were received by a cadaverous yet jocular gentleman sitting in the reception room, who, with much chortling and a roguish twinkle, directed us across to a lady colleague on the other side of the room. There was much ado as a collection of the most disreputable chairs imaginable was assembled for us in front of the said lady's desk.

With the utmost dignity, our Immigration lady summoned inkpad and rubber stamp and studied our forms carefully. She was intrigued by our boat's name 'Gone With The Wind', which she had never come across before. I tried to explain what it meant and that it was also the name of a very famous American film starring Clark Gable and Vivien Leigh. The old surreal, twilight zone feeling came over me again as I realised both she and the Port Captain did not have a clue what I was talking about. Gee, to think there is somewhere on earth where they have never heard of 'Gone With The Wind'! I refrained from humming the theme tune.

Eventually, after yet more paper shuffling and perusing of passports and consultations with our Captain, we obtained Immigration clearance at no charge—except that, through the Captain we were given to understand that the lady would be most appreciative of any old T-shirt that we might let her have! We readily agreed to the terms and hastened on to the bank to change some money, our Captain still firmly in tow.

We had just reached the gates of the bank building when a gentleman informed us that it was closed! Nothing to be done but return to the boat and come back the following day to complete our business. This we duly did and, upon changing US$160, found ourselves Malagasy Franc millionaires! At over FMg6000 to the dollar, we now seemed to have more money than we knew what to do with. The first chore was to settle up with the Port Captain and collect the receipt. The next chore was to hand over the promised T-shirt for our Immigration lady. Perhaps it was our warped sense of humour, but we could not resist giving her one which bore on the front the proud name of a yacht we had sailed on some years before: 'Shady Lady'! Anyhow, we hope she enjoyed it. Finally, it was set-tling-up time with the Customs official and there we ran into a snag when we found he did not have any change for our large banknotes. Nothing daunted, he opened a back window and summoned a ragged little boy to accompany us to the shops so that we could get the change and send it back to the Customs office via the little lad.

Back we marched along one of the two equally dusty roads towards the town centre with the boy in tow and filled with the strangest sensation that we had suddenly landed in a Clint Eastwood western—you know the one where the strangers meet in the main street for the final showdown! The gazes we attracted were not hostile, however. People were curious about us and friendly towards us and soon we were hailed by a dark, lanky, dreadlocked youth, who latched onto us as an unofficial tourist guide, claiming to speak both French and English. He was a bit optimistic on the English, for he could not seem to understand much of what we said, but his French was passable and we were able to communicate in that lan-guage. (Richard mentioned that one often gets latched onto in this way in the villages, that it is usually harmless and one should simply go along with it.) The name of our 'guide' was Eloi and he turned out to be a sweet and gentle youth, despite his rather outlandish appearance. First stop was the market, where we were ushered into what looked like a shack from the outside but turned out to be a delightful little bar-cum-shop, where we purchased some mineral water and got our change to send back to the Customs officer. Then we ended up in a more substantial building with a pleasant verandah bar, where we had some of the excellent local Three Horses Beer (THB, 'tay-ash-bay' or 'trois chevaux' as it is known).

Not surprisingly after generous glasses of beer, Don asked the way to the toilet. He was somewhat taken aback to find himself ushered into the dusty backyard of the establishment, where the 'toilet' took the form of just a bare corner of earth screened off by a fence of thin poles lashed together. Our Malagasy lavatorial education had only just begun! We were to discover that, not only are such bare earth arrangements quite normal amongst the local people, but some of the beaches are used in the same way. Presumably the Malgache work on the premise that when you have to answer a call of Nature, then Nature must take care of the detritus. Fortunately, the fairly substantial tidal range at Morombe helped to keep its beaches relatively unsullied. Nevertheless, it is not surprising that diseases like cholera still take their toll in Madagascar from time to time.

Soon we had to return to the boat, for we were to bring our washing ashore to be done at the Port Captain's office. Eloi accompanied us back to our dinghy, all the while telling us about each building we passed and the agricultural and fishing activities of the area. We were impressed at how neat the little traditional Malgache houses were, with their dusty yards enclosed by fences of thin poles. Everything was lashed together. Not a nail or screw was to be found anywhere. The ground was swept as clean as a new pin and not a piece of rubbish or a discarded plastic bag was to be seen. What a welcome sight that was for us after seeing what irresponsible consumerism can do to a country like South Africa and to many others! Here, the people lived close to nature. Why, even the fishing pirogues were not built of planks as western craft might be, but were painstakingly hollowed out of whole trunks of native trees, probably not so very differently from how the first men on earth fashioned their primitive craft. The girls had time to sit in the shade of trees and groom each other's hair for hours on end, creating the intricate braids and patterns that are such an important part of their culture.

We passed by the bank, one of the most imposing buildings in town apart from the Palais de Justice (the Court Building)—why is it that banks are always in magnificent buildings? Opposite, was an open area of more or less flat ground on which a crowd of youngsters were enthusiastically engaged in a game of basketball. According to Eloi, it was a very popular sport and the town took pride in its team, which it would send from time to time to compete with other teams at various levels.

At the far end of town we passed the local penitentiary, with the charmingly euphemistic title 'maison centrale'. Eloi informed us that this was where people caught stealing the local livestock were put. Goats, pigs, chickens, ducks and geese all seemed to wander around freely, so it was no doubt fairly easy to do a bit of 'rustling' on the sly! Having got onto the subject of livestock, Eloi told us that he kept goats and chickens. In fact, he offered to bring us a chicken—a live chicken! We protested vehemently that it was too kind of him and that we could not possibly have a live chicken on the boat, etc, but somehow he did not seem to understand. Eventually we parted company on the beach, agreeing to meet up with him the next day for a provisioning trip to the market.

For now, we had to take care of our washing and fill a few jerrycans of water. This we did at the concrete wash tubs in the back yard of the Port Captain's office, where Monsieur le Capitaine himself greeted us, once again suitably attired for the occasion in a pair of bright red bathing trunks. A gaggle of children ran around us and helped the Captain to fill the containers for us, while others sponged out our dinghy. As an even more helpful gesture, Madame the Captain's wife was volunteered to help with the washing. This she did with great thoroughness, instructing me how to do the hand-washing properly in her halting French. Women's work is the same the world over! We chatted as we worked. She told me that she and the Captain had 24 children! They lived in the little wood and palm-frond huts out behind the office, together with all the usual livestock and a poor, sandy vegetable patch where some sugar cane and tomato plants were making a valiant effort to survive. What could one say? 'Vingt-quatre enfants! Ça ç'est une grande famille.' It was only later that Don and I marvelled, with our western perceptions, at how people can survive with such large families. Well, at least the Captain had enough for two football teams, including the substitutes. Perhaps, we thought, someone should introduce him to 'hobbies' other than procreation!

After giving Madame some money as a recompense for her work, which she reluctantly but graciously accepted, we carted our washing back to the boat. Next chore was to buy some beer from the local wholesaler-cum-hotelier right by the beach. Malagasy beer is sold in 65cl bottles and there is a charge for the bottles and the 20-bottle crate. Here it worked out about R4 (60 US cents) a beer plus about R30 (US$4) for the crate and bottles. We duly carted the crate of beers back to the boat in what was by now a rather hairy dinghy-ride, with sizable waves whipped up over the shallows by the freshening afternoon breeze. All was well, however, and we soon had the beers safely stowed aboard, beneath our forward bunk. We were beginning to settle in nicely: beers in the fridge, washing done and whipping away on lines strung up fore and aft on deck, freshly-made bread.... Life was good. We saw Richard again and paid him for some diesel which he had kindly let us have out of his consignment from the local 'Solima' fuel depot. I also gave him one of my home-made loaves to thank him for all the help (not to mention all the beers) he had given us during our time here. His local knowledge had been invaluable.

It blew like stink all night and we were relieved to find all our washing still attached to our makeshift lines next morning. We watched the daily procession of dug-out pirogues, with square sails that looked as though they were made out of old rice sacks sewn together, making their way to the fishing grounds. They fairly whizzed along on the land breeze, delicately balanced on their outriggers and piloted by fishermen hunched forward like jockeys racing to the finishing post. They waved cheerily to us. Then it was breakfast and, with the sun risen enough to warm our cockpit slightly, time to bare all and take the morning 'bath' with a bucket of sea water. I went first and was just in the process of soaping up when the prow of a pirogue came into view alongside our boat. Then a big woolly hat appeared and dreadlocks and the grinning face of Eloi. Not only Eloi, but two of his friends and some things he had brought us: a small bag of shells he had collected and the live chicken! We managed to dissuade him from presenting us with the poor chicken, but he handed over the shells and we agreed to meet later in town.

When the tide had risen enough to enable us to land well up the beach, we set off once more in the dinghy. We landed by the Port Captain's place, where a whole football team of children greeted us and proceeded to help us haul the boat up, amid much chatter and laughter. We made our way towards the town centre and soon met up with Eloi. For the next few hours he took us in tow and we were able to get at least some of the provisions we needed. First we went to the 'boulangerie' (bakery), owned by an Indian according to Eloi, where we were ushered through a courtyard filled with golden-husked rice drying in the sun and into the barn-like bakery itself. Inside we found several Malagasy men, stripped to the waist and sweating in the heat from a mound of glowing embers in the middle of the floor, busily preparing long French loaves for the oven. In the far corner, some baked loaves were laid out to cool and we selected three of them, for which we paid the princely sum of 65 SA cents (9 US cents) each! Next we made our way to the local market, where we were able to buy a fairly limited supply of fresh fruit and vegetables. We took some tomatoes, carrots and oranges of reasonable quality at next to nothing in price. We could not find any fresh milk and the meat we saw lying exposed to the blazing sun and the flies we certainly gave a miss! Many of the stalls displayed the locally-grown rice and large white beans known as 'Pois du Cap', which are exported to Europe and the Far East. In the local shops we bought mineral water, orange juice and wheat flour for my bread-making. The latter was scooped from a large sack into a plastic bag which I had had the foresight to bring, again at next to nothing in price. It was marvellous stuff—and they did not charge extra for the 'livestock' it contained: large brown weevils, which not only provided excellent sport but also added a certain 'je ne sais quoi' of body to my loaves!

Thus re-provisioned, we set off in search of liquid refreshment in the form of Three Horses Beer, which we found at the delightful beach bar of the hotel La Pirogue D'Or (Golden Pirogue or 'Lakana Volimena' in

Malgache). Ourselves and Eloi were glad to rest our feet for a while under the whispering coconut palms and casuarinas. The bar itself was made out of a beautifully carved and painted pirogue and all around were items such as turtle shells, conch shells, the 'saw' from a sawfish and, taking pride of place, a small stuffed crocodile grinning devilishly at us from the bar counter! A TV in the corner was showing some incongruous French station with the latest hit records and computer graphics. It became evident that Eloi had no inkling of how such images are generated or how computers work. In fact, we had yet to see any evidence of computers at all here. The highest technology playthings in Madagascar are the wheel rims which the boys propel down the street with sticks! No computer games or amusement arcades here.

As we enjoyed the beer, Eloi told us a bit about his family. He was one of twelve children, his father was dead and his mother fully occupied at home looking after the youngest of the children. They all did what they could to keep the family going: keeping goats and chickens, growing produce to sell at the market, working inland in the rice plantations and, in Eloi's case, a bit of unofficial tourist-guiding and interpreting. He hoped eventually to get himself a camera and earn a living taking photos for identity documents. We asked whether there were not some government or other agencies that could help the local people out of their grinding poverty. Eloi smiled sadly. It seems the money is there, but somehow it always ends up in the pockets of the local officials, or at least that seems to be the general perception. As for the banks, they will only lend to people who have an account with them. Jobs in the civil and public services are few and far between, as are employment opportunities in the few local businesses, which are largely Indian or French-owned.

There was obviously some animosity between the ordinary Malgache people and those they considered to be the wealthy merchant class, particularly the Indians. Perhaps if the Malgache studied carefully what it is that makes the Indians and others so successful in business, they might be able to lift themselves out of the mire a little. To start with, reducing the size of the average family would undoubtedly help. (Easy enough for us to say, I suppose). As Richard explained to us, in these little fishing villages there is nothing much to do but eat fish and rice and make babies! As soon as they are able, the youngsters start making babies and then there is nothing to be done but go out fishing so they can sell a few fish at the market to give them a little money to buy rice to eat with the fish. Such is the life of the average fisherman of the Vezo tribe who inhabit this coast. We marvelled all the more at how polite and cheerful they all are amid the appalling poverty.

Eloi really laid on the sob story about how his younger brothers and sisters depended on him to bring in a little money so they could eat. We gave him a bit of money in recompense for his work as our guide. In addition, I gave him two French coins which I had found amongst our things on the boat and which he had indicated were the latest fashion accessory for the young people to hang around their necks. After exchanging addresses, we made our way back to our dinghy where, surrounded by the smiling gaggle of Captain's children, we shook hands and said our farewells. We putted back to our boat, waving at the ever-smiling crowd on the beach until they receded, dispersed and went their separate ways.

We had no sooner got aboard our boat, when Richard and a local girl called Nirina came by. We invited them on board and spent a pleasant hour or two chatting and joking over beers and snacks. Richard was highly amused by the story of the live chicken. According to him, all you have to do is hang the bird up by the feet over a basin, cut off its tongue and it will quietly bleed to death without any fuss. That still leaves the plucking and cleaning, which for city slickers like us remains a mystery—we can only deal with the ready-prepared chicken that comes from the hypermarket! Richard remarked that the local chickens have very long legs and he reckoned this was because they belong to the breed that is used for cock-fighting. Nirina looked a bit doubtful, but Richard said yes, the locals enjoy betting on such activities. In fact, he recounted having been 'taken to the cleaners' just playing a friendly game of cards with Nirina's friends and sisters one day!

Soon it was time for them to leave, but not before Richard had given us much useful information about anchorages along this stretch of coast and much encouragement to explore this area more deeply. He had a real love for Madagascar, having immersed himself in the culture to the extent that he was welcomed in many villages and could sit down with the tribal elders or go off into the bush with them to hunt wild boar for days at a time. A real character was Richard, and a true Frenchman in his sense of individuality and adventure. We enjoyed our time with him very much.

Morombe To The Barren Islands

▼

On 30 June we left Morombe en route for the Barren Islands, some 180 miles north. After breakfast, our radio schedule with other yachtspeople and farewells to Richard, we weighed our tandem anchors and set sail. By late morning, we were through the pass in the reef, and with a final wave to the fishermen bobbing on their pirogues, we turned our faces towards our next destination.

The coastline is low, scrubby and featureless here, but offshore lie fairly shallow banks with intriguing names like Coelacanth Banks and Cachalot (Whale) Banks. I discovered how aptly named the latter were when I turned and caught a glimpse of a large, dark whale briefly surfacing and diving astern of us. We gazed for ages but could not see him again. The only indication of his presence was the entourage of wheeling seabirds in the air above the boiling ocean. We soon discovered why there was such a concentration of birds and sea mammals here—fish galore. Don got his fishing rod out and trolled a lure over our stern. Within minutes he got a bite and when he reeled in the line he found the lure and the weight completely gone! Then he tried a hook with a bit of bread and within moments he caught a small bonito, which we cooked and ate for supper, grateful of a respite from tinned food.

We must have offended old Neptune, for that night the wind piped up to over 30 knots from the east and the sea became very rough. It remained quite unpleasant for much of the next day and was very wearing on our stamina. The GPS said we were coming abeam of the port of Morondava, but in these conditions it did not look as though we would obtain much shelter there and we decided to press on. By evening, the wind had moderated enough to allow Don to try his luck again with the fishing rod. Within moments, he had hooked another bonito, but in trying to reel it in he managed to break the reel and lose the fish into the bargain! Shortly afterwards he had occasion to drop a bucket overboard to collect some sea water and claimed to have seen a huge fish swim into and then out of the bucket before he could haul it aboard.

That night, just north of Morondava, we saw the lights of a large fishing vessel close by. He hailed us on radio and we had a lengthy conversation in a French that was not helped by my lack of technical jargon nor his blood/Pastis level! He was definitely a Frenchman and it was all rather fun. At last, I managed to fathom out that he was going to come around behind us and start trawling beside us on our port side. He assured us that we would be in no danger and would not have to alter our course for him. He was highly amused by our name 'Gone With The Wind'—he had obviously cottoned onto the significance and it was a relief to find we had returned to some kind of cultural normality, albeit a rather boozy one! Monsieur le Pêcheur warned us that we would encounter other fishing vessels up ahead on our way to the Barren Islands. He was not wrong and by the early hours, off Cape Kimby, we found ourselves surrounded by several large, but thankfully stationary, blips on the radar screen, which we watched like a hawk until we were safely past and clear.

This was just one of several instances where we were very grateful for our radar. We had acquired this piece of fairly expensive and power-hungry equipment after hearing a salutary story from one of our yachting friends, who had had the unenviable experience of being run down by a ship in mid-Atlantic! He and his girlfriend had been sailing north from the island of St Helena in bad weather, with poor visibility. He did not have radar, but did have a small device which gave a warning signal if any radar-using vessel came into his vicinity. He came up on watch and peered all around into the murky, rain-drenched night. Nothing to be seen. Then he heard the sound of a ship's engine very close by, but there was no signal on the warning device and no sign of any vessel.

Understandably agitated by now, he looked all round, then he looked up.....just in time to see the massive bows of a ship looming above him out of the murk. There was no time to do anything but hang on and pray. The ship was moving on a collision course at right angles to the yacht and it ploughed straight over it, pushing it under the keel. Fortunately, the yacht missed the ship's propellers and bobbed up to the surface, but not without mortal damage to hull and mast. The yacht probably only survived because it was made of steel and not fibreglass. Our friend was also quite badly injured and was very worried about his girlfriend who was still below decks. Thankfully, she was unhurt and managed to pass up the emergency 'grab bag' (which all yachtsmen keep handy in case they have to abandon ship), in which there was a spare hand-held VHF radio. Our friend immediately sent a 'mayday' distress message. Two unexpected things happened: the warning device suddenly activated, indicating that the ship had only then switched its radar on, and the ship slowed and began to turn back towards the yacht.

The ship was from one of the Baltic states, formerly part of the USSR. It was bound from South America to Zaire (The Congo) in Africa. Miraculously, it had picked up the mayday and was coming back to rescue the pair it had just run down and take their stricken yacht in tow. As soon as he got aboard, our friend discovered why his warning device only activated *after* he sent his mayday: the ship's owners were too poor to allow it to use its radar, except in a dire emergency! The crew were living on the bones of their backsides, with nothing but cabbage and salt pork to live on for the whole voyage. Even their medical kit was poor in comparison with the yacht's, which prompted them to go aboard her and salvage a number of things before, sadly, the old girl succumbed to her injuries and sank beneath the Atlantic swells. It was a heartbreaking moment for our friend. He had put such a lot of work and love into her.

However, of more pressing concern was where they were going to end up. Our friend did not relish landing in a hospital in Zaire in the midst of the civil war that was raging at the time. He managed to contact family and yacht club friends and he and his girlfriend were eventually flown back to South Africa via a circuitous route which involved a helicopter ride to an oil-rig off the Angolan coast. Nothing daunted, as soon as he had recovered from his injuries, he went right out and bought another yacht, which, as far as I am aware, he and his girlfriend are still cruising in to this day. The first thing we did after hearing his story was to go out and buy ourselves a radar! Modern yacht radar is easy to use and enables the yachtsman to set up a 'safety zone' around his vessel, with an audible warning if anything strays into the zone. Although radar is power-hungry in continuous operation, one can save power by having the radar periodically switch itself on, make a few sweeps and then switch itself off again. Time and again we found it absolutely indispensable in conditions of restricted or zero visibility.

At first light, we were hailed on VHF radio by South African yacht 'Fujimo', a steel Barens Seatrader sloop, which had spent the night hove to in the vicinity of the fishing fleet (presumably because they didn't have radar!). We discovered that 'Fujimo' is an acronym which involves a certain gentleman called Jack and something about 'I'm movin' on'! They had come to Madagascar from Richards Bay via Europa Island and, like us, were in the process of exploring the coast, with next stop the Barren Islands. It was nice to have some company, and we sailed along in tandem until we reached the first of the Barren Islands, Nosy Lava. There we dropped anchor off the northern side of the island, while 'Fujimo' pottered on doing a bit of fishing and ended up anchored off the neighbouring island of Nosy Andrano, just a mile or two away. After doing some snorkelling in disappointingly cloudy water, we decided to head across to

Nosy Andrano, where we were assured the water was very clear and there was some good snorkelling to be had.

The folks on 'Fujimo' were right. We spent a lovely two days there, exploring the island and the magnificent fringing reefs. The colours and varieties of coral, shells and fish were a delight, and the clear water shaded from midnight blue to teal to pale bottle green. I discovered two sting rays lying nose to nose in a patch of sand, trying to look inconspicuous, their long curving tails spread out behind them. I watched them at a respectful distance, not wanting to annoy them or spoil an exquisite moment. As the tide went out, a treasure trove of marine life was left stranded in the pools amongst the hummocks of exposed coral. I found a small ray, brown with bright blue spots, trying to hide in the sand. Local fishermen, who had a camp on the island, were also exploring the reefs and every so often we would hear shouts of glee as one of them would spear an octopus and brandish it aloft as a trophy.

Our new friends on 'Fujimo', George and Mary and crewmen Louis and Jay, were very kind to us and supplied us with lots of the beautiful fish which they had been catching. We had braaied (barbecued) fish, pickled fish, curried fish and smoked fish—in fact, fish till it was coming out of our ears, but it was so fresh and delicious that we never got tired of it! We also got some fishing tips from these seasoned fishermen.

It was a beautiful spot, within sight of mainland Madagascar, surrounded by tropical islands with beaches of pale coral sand. Unfortunately, being exposed to the prevailing easterly and south-easterly monsoon winds of that time of year, it was a very bouncy anchorage. Interesting for those looking to spice up their sex-life perhaps, but extremely uncomfortable for sleeping! Despite the bounciness, we found it a secure anchorage in 5-9m of water, in good holding sand and the occasional clump of coral. The Malagasy fishermen would greet us as they went by on their way to the reefs, but otherwise they left us in peace, except for one enterprising chap who paddled out one night in a tiny canoe, with a skinny little lad holding up an enormous blue lobster that was almost as big as he was. The daunting logistics of preparing such a sea monster and Don's aversion to crustacea prompted me to direct them over to 'Fujimo', where I knew Monsieur Langouste would be received with relish! Before you could say Jacques Robinson, the lobster was hauled aboard in a bucket, undoubtedly destined for 'Fujimo's' capacious braai.

Barren Islands To Baly Bay

▼

On 4 July we left the beautiful Nosy Andrano in the Barren Islands and continued our voyage up the west coast of Madagascar towards a large natural harbour called Baly Bay or 'Helodrano Baly' as it is known in the Malagasy language. It was a trip of just over 200 miles and we had fairly light to moderate winds from just about every direction along the way. For much of the way we also had 'Fujimo' for company and it was fun chatting to them on radio. Although we were well used to it by now, sailing with just two people on board can be a bit tedious, especially through the long watches of the night. We fell into a routine of three hours on/three hours off, which suited us quite well, but nevertheless fatigue always made its presence felt after a while. In true cruising fashion, we were always quite happy to reach the next anchorage and catch up on lost sleep.

On the first night out, in the early hours of the morning en route to Baly Bay, we had something of a thunderstorm, with some exciting squally winds, but we came through it unscathed and enjoyed mainly downwind sailing from then on. The next day, we rounded Cape St André, again in the early hours of the morning, with a lovely 20 knot south-easter, and set course for Baly Bay. There were many fishing vessels in the area and one of them came quite close to 'check us out', hailing us on VHF radio and asking us all sorts of questions in execrable English, accompanied by long 'aaahs' and 'yohs' that would have gone down well in Japanese Noh

Theatre. It turned out he was Taiwanese, as he explained very carefully to me as if I were some idiot child. All I could do was wish him luck with the fishing: 'bonne chance', 'bonne pêche', etc, and off he steamed, quite happy to have had some funny foreigners with whom to while away a boring half-hour or so! They always like to talk to the lady on board and get just about your entire family history. I'm convinced it must be their version of a soap opera!

As we approached Baly Bay, Don managed to hook a magnificent barracuda—must have been around ten pounds—using heavy line, bungee cord and a piece of plastic bag as a lure, but as he tried to gaff the fish and bring him aboard he got away! So disappointing! Ah well, the luck of the fisherman. At least we were within sight of a safe and peaceful anchorage. Baly Bay was indeed a natural harbour, with fine protecting headlands of the most beautiful coloured rock strata, clothed in almost primeval forest. We anchored in under 4 metres of water on the west side of the bay, just off a deserted beach. What a difference from our previous anchorages! It was so calm and sheltered.

However, we were to learn a valuable lesson the next day when we discovered to our horror that we were crunching on the bottom at low tide. The water level had fallen by around three metres and we were in danger of being stranded once again! We got the engine going and managed to creep into deeper water, where we re-anchored and spent the rest of our stay there without incident. One must always make allowances for a considerable fall of the tide here, especially in shallow bays. We spent a day just resting, relaxing, cleaning the boat and doing some laundry. 'Fujimo' arrived and we listened, with amusement, to their progress up the bay to the small settlement of Baly, in search of fuel, water and cigarettes (for one of their crewmen). We asked Mary what Baly was like—was it a one-horse town?—and she described it as a 'half-horse town', so we kind of got the picture! We were not sure if they managed to get the water or fuel, but the cigarette-seeking crewman came back quite happy, apparently.

BALY BAY TO MAJUNGA (MAHAJANGA)

————————▼————————

With fresh foods, water and fuel dwindling, we decided to make for the major port of Majunga, some 60 miles up the coast, where we hoped to re-provision. We left at 0-dark-thirty on 8 July and, with the cool breath of the land breeze behind us, we motor-sailed out of Baly Bay between the headlands known as Tanjona Amparafaka and Tanjona Sada, heading north-east. The velvet heavens and sea were illuminated by the glow of a million stars. Directly ahead, as if to guide us, was the exquisite cluster known as the Pleiades, and there on the eastern horizon the familiar outline of Orion, rising magnificent out of the sea.

The sun rose majestically behind the next headland of Tanjona Tanjo, just as dramatic with its coloured rock strata as those we had left behind. The wind did not cooperate, however, and we had light to moderate north-easterlies on the nose for much of the day. However, with the incoming tide, we had a favourable current of up to a knot pushing us along and we made good progress. We motor-sailed until about midday, when the wind began freeing off to the north, allowing us to get out the full mainsail and roller-furling genoa. We were sailing once again. Around us were several fishing vessels and local pirogues going about their business. The coastline is fairly featureless here, except for a rather magnificent off-lying island called Nosy Makamby, which from a distance looks just like the outline of Table Mountain, with Signal Hill and Devil's Peak on either side. Just as we came abeam of it, we found ourselves overhauling a large dhow-like sailing craft, with smiling, waving Malgache crew, which added even more charm to the scene. It was like stepping back into history: the vessel looked like the ship that Vasco Da Gama used on his voyages of exploration over 500 years ago. No doubt Arab traders were plying this coast in such vessels for very much longer than that.

Our Malgache sailing vessel could not keep as close to the wind as we could. He fell off and headed slightly more inshore of us, but he kept up a good speed and stayed right on our heels all the way to Majunga. We could not help wondering whether the racing spirit had got into the crew and they were tweaking the controls here and there to try to outpace the vazahas' yacht! It was great fun, anyway. The conditions were perfect and we arrived in the port of Majunga by early evening, amid a swarm of homecoming fishing pirogues all heading into the enormous Bombetoka Bay. By 5.45pm we were anchored off the small craft harbour, just in time to admire the glorious sunset through the waving palms on the Pointe de Sable, with its slightly run-down colonial mansions forming the Port Captain's premises.

Majunga! Fascinating mixture of Third World and faded French colonial grandeur. We had heard all kinds of alarming stories about past conflicts between the Malgache and Comorian and other foreign immigrants; about violence and thieving. It was here that Richard had once had his dinghy and outboard stolen from behind his yacht, while he and his crew were asleep on board! We had been warned so often about being careful here that we locked ourselves in our boat at night as securely as Fort Knox! We had had a set of stainless steel 'burglar bars' made in Durban and these we slotted into the main hatch and secured with a padlock. It meant that the solid wooden parts of the hatch could be left open, allowing the air to circulate below decks, essential in the tropics.

We decided on the burglar bars after hearing about a violent robbery suffered by a South African couple on a yacht identical to ours in St Vincent in the Caribbean. In a nightmare scenario, the wife was murdered, the husband accused of the crime and jailed and then only released on payment of a substantial sum of money. He was vindicated later when South African detectives went out to St Vincent and actually tracked down the real perpetrators, who still had incriminating evidence on them. However, in our case we need not have worried. We found ourselves to be completely safe and met with nothing but friendly greetings and flashing white smiles in the black faces of the local seafaring folk.

Majunga is a bustling port, whose main exports are seafood and raffia. Several sizable ships were anchored in Bombetoka Bay when we arrived, waiting for their containers to be unloaded and ferried to the quay by barge. There was also quite a fleet of fishing vessels and traditional Malgache trading vessels, similar to the one we had 'raced' on our way here. 'Boutres' they are called. They have no engines, which makes it extremely difficult for them to get into or out of the small craft harbour. They often have to claw their way forward with anchors and lines. In fact, one day we helped one of them get a tow line ashore so that it could be hauled out against a head wind. We marvelled at the infinite patience and seamanship of these 'boutre' sailors, armed only with sail and muscle-power.

After a peaceful night on anchor, we went ashore in our dinghy. As we putted into the small craft harbour, we were surprised to find some yachts amongst the trading vessels, one of which bore a South African flag! It was an ex-Durban catamaran called 'Zwilling', now owned, as we were to discover, by a charming Frenchman called Guy. He hailed us as we approached and told us to tie our dinghy up on his stern. His young Malgache 'gardien' (watchman) would keep an eye on it for us! Before we had a chance to thank Guy, he was gone, but his young employee made us feel quite at home. He was a delightful young man, always eager to help, speaking good French and always with a warm smile on his face. He was nattily dressed too, with his smart T-shirt and back-to-front baseball cap: he could have passed for Will Smith's younger brother! His name was Dex, and he took his job seriously and made quite sure our dinghy and outboard engine were entirely safe while we explored the town.

No sooner had we set foot on dry land, when we were taken in tow by another enterprising youth named Augustin who pulled an intriguing rickshaw-like contraption known here as a 'pousse-pousse' (so named in the days when they were propelled by two men, one pushing at the back and the other pulling from in front, yelling 'pousse, pousse!' all the time.) First stop was the market: 'le grand marché' or 'bazaaribe'. Augustin was a lovely lad. He could not speak very much French, but he tried very hard and he looked after us as if he owned us. We went into a small café, where we had two 'café au laits' in order to get enough change to pay Augustin. This was where we discovered that 'café au lait' is very strong filter coffee served with sweetened condensed milk! Yucch! Yet after the first few sips it becomes almost palatable. We wandered around the area for a bit and were accosted by another pousse-pousse driver who tried to take us in tow. Eventually, Augustin rescued us and helped us with our shopping in the market.

We found the traders somewhat more enterprising than those we had encountered in Morombe, having a good range of fresh produce and even some plastic carrier bags for their customers. We could tell we were in the big city now! Eggs, milk and meat were also available, although the hygiene conditions did nothing to encourage us to try the latter. At a nearby grocer's we found Liquifruit orange juice, but it was only when we got it back to the boat that we discovered it was months beyond its sell-by date and only fit for cooking with. However, there was nothing wrong with the freshness of the baguettes and sweet pastries we found at the local boulangerie (bakery). Then, for the equivalent of R2.50 (35 US cents) Augustin delivered us back to the Port au Boutres (small craft harbour).

It is impossible to explain what it is like riding in a pousse-pousse to someone who has never tried it. It is as strange and uncanny a feeling to be pulled along by a human being running between the shafts like a horse as it is to imagine what it must be like to have to earn your living that way. The only saving grace about the whole thing is that at least it gives some of these poor devils a job.

After a lunch of omelettes, salad, French bread and pastries aboard 'Gone With The Wind', we felt our stamina sufficiently restored to dinghy our way into the small craft harbour once again. However, one peek around the breakwater revealed that the tide had gone out and the little harbour was rapidly drying, revealing an oozing and odoriferous quagmire across which we had no desire to venture. The faithful Dex was ready for us and signalled us alongside a ferry boat which was tied up on the outside of the breakwater. We were the object of much interest and solicitous attention from the Captain and crew, who were so concerned about the safety of our dinghy that they even offered to haul it on board. However, with Dex on guard, we knew it would be fine.

We walked around town for a bit, but as it was a Sunday virtually all the shops were closed. We ended up at a delightful open-air café called the 'Cap Ouest' on the Pointe de Sable waterfront, overlooking our anchorage. We sat at one of an impressive set of rustic tables, which incorporated an elaborate roof and built-in benches, and observed our fellow-customers. They were a disparate mix of pale-skinned European holidaymakers, local families enjoying a Sunday outing and a group of military men in uniform. Our beers arrived and were no sooner opened when we were beset by flies, a persistent and ubiquitous menace in a country where livestock roams freely and sanitation leaves a lot to be desired. However, the people around us were charming. The Malgache women are quite beautiful in their traditional garb and even the youngsters exhibit a certain Gallic reserve and self-assurance. In this atmosphere of calm, it was impossible to imagine the bloodthirsty days of 1977 when around a thousand Comorians, mainly illegal immigrants, were slaughtered on the streets of Majunga amidst bitter fighting.

We spent 4 days at Majunga. Our Frenchman, Guy, was kind enough to help us with the diesel fuel, which we found had to be obtained from a filling station in the middle of town. He transported us in his 4x4 vehicle out to his self-built, Moroccan-style house overlooking the sea, where we enjoyed a beer and picked up an extra jerrycan which he lent us. That, together with our container, enabled us to ferry enough fuel out to the boat to top up our tank quite nicely. According to Guy, he had received such kindness in South Africa that his assistance to us was just by way of repayment. He was a fascinating character, having been born and brought up in Morocco when it was still a French colony and then living and working in many other French overseas territories.

He had no illusions about human nature: yes, the Malgache are very sweet, very charming…but thieves! Aside from such observations, he gave us much useful information: that no fuel or fresh water is available between Majunga and Nosy Be; that provisions are three times the price in Nosy Be; that you cannot trust the charts of Madagascar because they are very old and depths shown are unreliable, therefore always watch your depth-sounder when navigating in these coastal waters. He also indicated good anchorages on the coast and places worth a visit.

Much of the time a strong south-easterly wind swept in across the wide fetch of Bombetoka Bay and our boat fairly danced around on her anchor, making it quite uncomfortable for us. Going ashore in the dinghy could also be uncomfortable and usually left us with wet bottoms and feet. Mosquitoes and flies were surprisingly persistent at finding their way on board, even against the howling wind, and ashore we were occasionally assailed by a ferocious kind of horse-fly that lurked in sandy areas. Taking on fresh water turned out to be a very tedious business as there was only one outlet, situated on the main quay where ferries and fishing boats tied up. We brought 'Gone With The Wind' over and rafted up against a small coastal trading vessel, then spent the whole afternoon waiting in line to haul aboard a large, grubby canvas hose with which to fill our water tanks.

Hanging around the docks was quite an education. We watched with fascination and not a little apprehension as a huge herd of the local humped Zebu cattle were loaded onto a Comorian ferry boat. It was pandemonium on the quayside as herd boys ran around trying to manoeuvre the agitated beasts by whacking them with sticks and hauling on their tails, whilst staying out of range of their lethal-looking horns. With a colossal effort, each beast had to be cajoled to the top of a ramp which ran steeply down into the bowels of the ship. Then several herdsmen would push in unison on the hindquarters and the beast would slide unceremoniously down the ramp, landing with a sickening crump at the bottom.

When we returned to our boat after watching this diversion, we found we had attracted the attention of a dapper gentleman accompanied by some armed guards. He introduced himself as the dock manager and asked why we had not been to see him or the Port Captain. We explained that we had obtained our 3-month permit from the Port Captain of Morombe and we understood we were covered for all ports in Madagascar. Ah, but we should have checked in at the Port Captain's office here. He shook his head ruefully. What to do? Then he brightened a little and asked whether we might not perhaps have some cartons of cigarettes on board. We could see he was angling for a hand-out, but we explained we do not smoke and had no cigarettes on board. So he gave up, wished us a good day and went on his way.

We got our water tanks filled and then cast off from the little trading vessel. Immediately there were cries of dismay and several of her crew grabbed onto our boat, threatening to crunch us against the other vessel's steel topsides. It was money they wanted. We were outraged by their behaviour, but submitted and threw them what little change we had in order to prevent damage to our boat. We got away from there as quickly as possible, returning to the relative safety of our anchorage.

With fuel and water topped up, we concentrated on getting a few provisions. We discovered a small supermarket called 'Super G.A.' near the docks and in the same street as the cathedral. Staff there were friendly and prices and selection of goods were reasonable. Otherwise it was a long trek around the myriad small shops and the fresh produce market. Shopping is made more difficult by the long siesta in the middle of the day, when virtually everything closes between 12.30 and 2.30 or even 3pm. It was very frustrating. Then we found the local banks would not change US$100 bills (due to the prevalence of forgeries). The other obstacle to overcome was the appalling state of some of the roads and pavements. They had been tarred at one time, but most had large potholes, around which the local taxis navigated with verve. No doubt that was why the Europeans, Indians and Arabs who live in Majunga all tended to drive fancy 4x4 vehicles. You had to be careful where you walked, as there were gaping holes in the pavements, or open drains running alongside or places where piles of rubbish were being burned. There is no such thing as rubbish collection in Madagascar: you either burn it or recycle what you can of it. The poorer folk are always delighted to get your discarded bottles and cans for use as receptacles.

We sent postcards from the main post office in the centre of town. We found postage expensive, at R3-R4 (40-60 US cents) per card. We had heard that the postal service was none too reliable, with cases of customers' cash sometimes ending up in the pockets of the counter clerks! We were advised always to watch the clerk actually stick the stamp on the card. Telephoning was also quite an expensive business. The telecommunications office (AGATE) was next door to the main post office and sold telephone cards up to a value of R60 (US$8.60). For this you got 3-4 minutes when calling overseas. The public telephones were of the modern push-button type, but there were only two of them outside the AGATE office, and queues could be lengthy.

On our last day in Majunga, we had a pleasant lunch at a little restaurant called 'La Flibuste', near the small craft harbour. Guy had recommended it. For the equivalent of R103 (US$15) for the two of us, we had enormous helpings of wild boar paté, followed by Châteaubriand steak for Don and sea turtle fillet for me, accompanied by beer and a local 'gris' wine rather like a rosé. The 'patron', a big burly Frenchman, was a real one-man-show, and his dainty little Malgache waitresses were very sweet. It was the first time I had ever eaten turtle and I found it rather like a cross between chicken and fish. Interesting to try, but I am not sure I would have it again. Thus our stay at Majunga came to an end and we looked forward eagerly to the next stage of our voyage.

Majunga (Mahajanga) To Moramba Bay

▼

On the morning of 13 July, we set sail for Moramba Bay, some 75 miles up the coast. The steady south-easterly monsoon wind sped us on our way, past the long golden beach of Amborovy and the striking eroded red cliffs. Several fishing vessels were about, taking advantage of the rich harvest proffered by the shallow banks, which extend up to 20 miles offshore here. However, by afternoon the barometer had dropped and the wind had shifted until it was on the nose, so we had to motor-sail for a bit. By sunset, we were abeam Ankobohobo, some 30 miles north of Majunga, a good sheltered anchorage in a river mouth protected by sandbanks, which Guy had recommended.

We pressed on, and by late evening the wind had veered easterly and increased to 17-23 knots, with a choppy sea. We passed the entrance to Mahajamba Bay, another of the fine natural harbours which abound on this coast. There were some very shallow patches to cross and many fishing vessels about. By midnight, the easterly had strengthened to 20-27 knots and the sea had grown very rough. Then we found that our GPS was no longer showing a position and could not seem to locate any satellites. It was back to navigating by dead reckoning, and our radar came into its own, showing the distinctive coastal features of this area. After two hours, our GPS picked up some satellites and began displaying a position for us again.

By first light on 14 July, we found ourselves off the entrance to Moramba Bay. As daylight grew, we made our way in slowly and looked for a good spot to anchor. The wind was still howling from an easterly to south-easterly direction, so we had to seek out a sheltered cove on the south side. Later that morning, when the wind had died down, we moved to a beautiful spot in a small bay on the north side. Moramba Bay was an amazing natural harbour, full of delightful sandy coves and weird, eroded rocks, covered in dense vegetation. There were huge baobab trees, some coppery brown and others stark grey; there were also euphorbias and many other indigenous trees and shrubs. Bright green luxuriant mangroves fringed some parts of the shoreline.

The dramatic rocks and rocky islands had all been eaten away underneath by the water, so that at low tide they looked like gigantic mushrooms, and on top were perched all these enormous trees, clinging by their very roots to the bare rock. In some places, the rocks were weathered into jagged points, 'tsingys' as they are known in Madagascar. It was altogether an intriguing place.

In the late afternoon, we took a tour around in our rubber dinghy to view the rocks and islets more closely. They were wild and beautiful, quite awe-inspiring. We found fish eagles and kites perched in the trees and soaring in the air, hunting their prey. Then a whole troupe of black and white lemurs (ruffed lemurs or sifaka lemurs perhaps) came swinging, leaping and chattering through the branches of the baobabs. We watched them from our dinghy as we bobbed in a small inlet between the jagged rocks. They stopped and watched us, their babies clinging to their mothers' fur. Then it was time to break the spell and return to our boat. We had quite lost track of time and distance and ended up running out of petrol, so we had to paddle most of the way back, arriving as the sun dipped down towards the western horizon.

As the lustrous shades of sunset began to die away, a perfect full moon rose in the east and cast her silvery glow on yet more creatures of this enchanted place: dolphins. Always welcome visitors, the members of this particular school swam around our boat and then went on their way, exploring our little bay. These dolphins were of a distinctive hump-backed variety, with the dorsal fin set right in the middle of the hump. We were to encounter this type of dolphin several times during our cruise on the Madagascar coast.

We spent a peaceful night in this lovely anchorage. Our only regret about Moramba Bay was that due to the fresh winds the water was somewhat turbid and did not invite a great deal of swimming, except amongst the rocky islets, where it was perfectly clear and calm. All too soon, it was time to move on to our next destination, Nosy Saba and the Radama Islands.

MORAMBA BAY TO NOSY SABA
AND THE RADAMA ISLANDS

▼

We set off fairly early on the morning of 15 July, passing a large fancy cata-maran which must have come in either late the previous evening or early in the morning and was neatly tucked in the next cove, almost completely hidden by the rocks. There was no sign of life on board. By 8.30am, we were sailing out of Moramba Bay, past more of the weird mushroom rocks that stood like sentinels on one side of the entrance.

We enjoyed perfect sailing conditions: a south-easterly, switching to north-westerly, 9-17 knots. With our full mainsail and genoa our boat speed was touching 6½ knots at times. The scenery was becoming more interesting, more rugged and hilly, with large boulders and eroded cliffs. About 15 miles north of Moramba Bay, we passed the entrance to the enormous inlet known as Narendry Bay. We began to see several islands up ahead and some mountainous scenery on shore.

By mid-afternoon, we passed the island of Nosy Lava, infamous as the place where some yachtspeople from South Africa were murdered some years ago by escaped prisoners from Madagascar's maximum security prison, which is situated there. It is a sizable island, some 5 miles long, covered in rolling hills and displaying many pale, eroded cliffs and rocky headlands. There were also some attractive sandy beaches, fringed with palm trees and dotted with some small huts. On one of the hills stood an old lighthouse with a cluster of other buildings around it, and on another hill there was a structure which looked rather like a watchtower. We wondered if this had anything to do with the prison. From a distance all looked peaceful and quite inviting, but we gave it a miss all the same!

By sunset, we arrived at the island of Nosy Saba, some 35 miles north of Moramba Bay, a tiny jewel set in a turquoise sea. We dropped anchor about 100m off a white sand beach, in 5-6m of water. There we found shelter from the north-westerly wind and absolute peace. As the full moon rose high above the crystal clear water, its light penetrated right down to the sea bed, illuminating the pale sand and patches of dark weed below us. Just 9 miles north of the dreaded Nosy Lava and around 3½ miles offshore we had found a little piece of paradise! Next morning we snorkelled on the fringing reefs and enjoyed an incredible variety of tropical fish and corals. We particularly liked the giant clams, sea anemones, square-shaped puffer fish and two vividly-striped lion fish hiding their fearsome spines under a clump of coral close to the beach. It was an effort to pull ourselves away, but by late morning we said farewell to our perfect 'desert island' and set sail for the Radama Islands.

There are four islands in the Radama group: Valiha, Antany Mora, Ovy and Kalakajoro, scattered around the beautiful and mountainous Berangoma Peninsula. We anchored overnight at Nosy Valiha, some 12 miles or so north of Nosy Saba. It was there that we saw a strange and beautiful sight: a partial eclipse of the full moon as it rose over the sleeping mountains of Madagascar. In the atmosphere of perfect calm and solitude we might have been the only people alive on earth. It was altogether a most picturesque spot, but unfortunately the water was not clear and did not tempt us to go snorkelling. We left the next day, 17 July, and motor-sailed in light variable winds past the other Radama Islands, which are fairly hilly and thickly wooded. From palm-fringed beaches and reefs, our eyes were drawn to the blue-grey mountains of Madagascar, sharply outlined in the morning light before the clouds started to gather and obscure their summits. It was a tantalising foretaste of the dramatic and beautiful scenery awaiting us as we voyaged north.

RADAMA ISLANDS TO NOSY IRANJA

▼

Fairly light north-westerly to northerly winds dominated as we made our way north from the Radama Islands on 17 July. In the middle of the day, we encountered the first yachts that we had seen for quite some time. They were both large charter catamarans, one called 'Bossi' and the other 'Coco de Mer', both heading south. We hailed each of them on VHF Channel 16 (the usual listening channel), but got no reply and shrugged it off as snootiness on their part until we discovered later that yachts around the Nosy Be area all keep their radios tuned to Channel 9! Despite not getting a reply from them, just seeing them gave us the pleasant, companionable feeling that, in yachting terms, we were somehow wandering back onto the beaten track again.

We arrived at Nosy Iranja, some 30 miles north of the Radama Islands, around 4pm and anchored in 4-7m of crystal clear water off the southwest tip of the smaller of two islands which form this exquisite place. Covered by lush vegetation and fringed by white coral sands, the smaller island is linked to the larger, rockier island by a sandspit which uncovers at low tide. 'Iranja' is the Malgache word for turtle, and there was certainly evidence of turtle nests on the beaches.

A resort hotel was just being completed on the smaller island: 'Nosy Iranja Islands-Dreams'. Its buildings are of traditional palm-frond and wood construction, well-concealed amongst the undergrowth. Guest accommodation is in individual huts overlooking the beaches, where for FF690 per person per night sharing (or FF1050 for a single) one can enjoy all mod cons, including air-conditioning, full board and use of water sports equipment. Transport from the airport on Nosy Be is an extra FF420 per person. They informed us they were hoping to provide a helicopter service soon, at a cost of over FF3000 per person! (The French Franc is virtually equivalent to the SA Rand.)

The patron and his staff made us very welcome at the hotel's attractive bar, set amongst the palms and tastefully furnished in cane and wood, with quaint roll-down blinds. Each large beer cost FMg10000 (R10), but it was worth it just to be able to relax in such a beautiful setting. The staff were very sweet and tried very hard to converse with us in English. They gave us the grand tour of the accommodation and it was very impressive.

We quite lost track of time and when we got back to our dinghy, we found that the rising tide had overwhelmed it and it was bobbing around in the surf. Fortunately, the anchor we had put out held, but one of our paddles was swept away and lost. Thankfully, we managed to get the outboard engine started and chugged back to the yacht, knee-deep in water and bailing furiously.

Whilst at Nosy Iranja, we met up with two Australian yachts: 'Jarlem' and 'Lizzy'. Their crews were very pleasant, real cruising people, and we exchanged information about places to visit. Both yachts were heading for South Africa and we hoped that we would meet up with them again there. Neither yacht remained overnight at Nosy Iranja, but headed across to Baramahamay Bay, on mainland Madagascar, where there is a sheltered anchorage in a wide river mouth. The cruising people had nicknamed it 'Honey River' because one could trade with the locals to obtain some of the beautiful wild honey to be found there.

We stayed for two nights at Nosy Iranja and the second night was one of our most uncomfortable ever! The effects of tidal streams, winds and a south-easterly swell made it very rolly. In fact, it was the first time I ever had to tie myself in the galley on anchor, in order to prepare our evening meal! It was unbelievable. We awoke bleary-eyed at first light the next day and it was a relief just to get going and get away from the rolling. However, in spite of the uncomfortable anchorage, we were not sorry we had taken the time to visit this lovely island.

NOSY IRANJA TO HELLVILLE, NOSY BE

▼

On 19 July, we motor-sailed the 30-odd miles to Hellville, in light variable winds and scorching hot sun, arriving by early afternoon. We were now in the far north-west of Madagascar, in the most popular cruising area, and it was not difficult to see why. The scenery was magnificent. All around were thickly-wooded mountains, islands, weird sugarloaf-shaped rocks and enormous bays. In one of the latter, Ambavatoby or 'Russian' Bay, we were delighted to discover 'Fujimo' and her crew again, for we heard them calling on radio.

However, we pressed on to Hellville, the capital and main port of Nosy Be (which means 'Big Island' in Malgache). There we found the largest number of yachts we had seen since we left Durban. There were French, German, Australian, New Zealand and South African yachts anchored in the harbour. There were also charter boats, both catamarans and monohulls, of all shapes and sizes, some of them very fancy-looking. After we found a suitable spot and dropped anchor, it did not take long for us to be assailed by the ubiquitous local 'boat boys', looking to guard our yacht and/or dinghy for us. We turned down the first kid who had come paddling over to our yacht and went ashore in our dinghy.

The only place to land is at the slipway where the inter-island ferries and trading boats dock. We no sooner set foot ashore when a crowd of yelling boat boys and taxi drivers battened upon us like a flock of starving vultures! We selected a lad called Michael, whose sole aim in life seemed to be to see how much he could wheedle out of the 'vazahas'. The going rate for looking after a dinghy for the day is FMg1000, but while you are away the boys generally make free with your dinghy and outboard, running around all over the harbour, unless you 'pull the plug' in some way to prevent it. The boys also try to get extra jobs cleaning your yacht and then of course they have a good look round to see if they can get T-shirts, caps or other 'presents' out of you. We were certainly grateful not to have our dinghy and/or outboard stolen (although others were not so lucky), but we came to dread the daily battle through the yelling mobs on the quayside which really put the 'Hell' in Hellville!

Hellville, or 'Andoany' as it is called in Malgache, is just another fairly scruffy port. It is considerably smaller than Majunga and, perhaps as a consequence, its roads are in considerably better repair—not that that is saying very much! However, it has a somewhat more prosperous air, with more tourists about, and there are some nice restaurants and bars. It was evident that there had been some investment in the town—largely French and Italian we were told. (Dark references to 'the Mafia' seemed to echo what our Frenchman, Guy, had told us in Majunga.)

The day after we arrived, we took a taxi and ran around getting provisions, butane gas for the stove and petrol for the outboard. The secret with the taxi drivers is to try to fix a price before you set off, as they inevitably inflate their tariffs for visitors. I am afraid though, try as we might, we never managed to pin one down to an agreed price and probably ended up paying three or four times the normal rate, although I must say it was always far less than one would expect to pay for the same distance in South Africa. The taxi drivers were also very obliging interpreters and porters when the need arose, and they would always wait patiently for us wherever our errands took us.

That day, we first went to an excellent 'cash and carry' in the main street, rather disconcertingly called the Rue de Hell but more recently renamed the Rue Passot, and replenished our beers at the equivalent of R3.50 (50 US cents) each—the cheapest yet and even cheaper than Majunga! Sadly, the 'cash and carry' closed down during the time we were there, but beers and other provisions were available at Le Chinois (or the Chinese Shop), opposite the market, at the same prices. Next to Le Chinois was a good-going money changing business run by a local from a pavement stall. He was a slick businessman, surrounded by muscular 'minders' who deterred any would-be thieves. His service was certainly a lot slicker than the bank, although at least they did not turn up their noses at $100 bills, as they had done at Majunga.

We had to call at the offices of 'Solima' to organise some butane gas. Ten kilos cost us R43 (US$6),which seemed reasonable, but then we discovered you have to drive all the way to the next settlement at Crater Bay to actually get the tank filled at the Solima depot! All we could do was sit back and enjoy the drive, although the roads occasionally deteriorated into some exciting potholes. At least it enabled us to see a little of the area.

The lush greenery we had seen while approaching Nosy Be from the sea turned out to be sugar cane plantations. There were also orchards of fruit trees and groves of coconut palms. There seemed to be no shortage of water. According to our taxi driver, it came from the many lakes up in the mountains. I asked him whether the land was still owned by the French and he said, no, it now belonged to the local people, but he did admit that many French and Italians had moved in to Nosy Be in recent years! We passed through little villages that were hives of cultivation and enterprise, with every second house having a little produce stall out front, or a small bar or shop. Beside the road ran a narrow-gauge railway, which our driver informed us was for the transportation of sugar cane. All around the scenery was attractively hilly and here and there we could make out the distinctive shapes of ancient volcanoes, in particular the one that gives Crater Bay its name.

After getting our gas bottle filled at Crater Bay, we returned to Hellville and paid a visit to the market. It seemed to us to be the best we had yet seen in terms of quality and variety, albeit a little more expensive than Majunga. Even the butchery section was not quite so off-putting! It must have lulled me into a false sense of complacency, for I found myself asking for chicken. An earnest gentleman led me all the way through to the rear of the market and proudly pointed to a pen of very much alive and squawky chickens, from which I was expected to make my selection! Oh dear, I'm afraid I 'chickened' out of that one, much to the amusement of the locals!

Instead, we returned to the butchery section and chose some already well and truly slaughtered meat from the local humped Zebu cattle, 'sans os' (without bones). It was very lean, slightly gamy and made an excellent curry when well-cooked in the pressure cooker. As our friend, Richard, had said in Morombe, the Malgache butchers are not familiar with the concept of 'hanging' the meat, no doubt understandable in this climate, and it tends to be a bit tough. It was delicious, though. Regarding the chicken, we discovered later that frozen chicken was available from Le Chinois, who proudly informed us that 'they had *everything*'. However, it was a bit disconcerting to thaw it out and find it came complete with feet and head, the latter gazing balefully at you with its beady little eyes! Like a character from a Stephen King novel, one had to push back an irrational image of the use to which all those chicken heads and feet were being put—voodoo, perhaps, or Chinese medicine?

As well as fresh produce, seafood and meat, there was an excellent spice market, where fragrant locally-grown items could be purchased at a fraction of the cost one could expect to pay in the West. I took a bundle of vanilla at the equivalent of R10 (US$1.40). When we got it back to the boat, it filled the interior with a strong and delightful aroma, like nothing that you would ever find in a western shop. Vanilla actually comes from a type of orchid and the whole pods can be used to flavour sauces, custard, ice cream and even the local Nosy Be rum, which when so treated produces a delicious liqueur.

After two days in Hellville, we were itching to get away from the crowds and the constant pestering of the boat boys. On 21 July, we left for the nearby island of Nosy Komba. The same day, a Government Minister from the Malgache capital, Antananarivo (or 'Tana for short), visited Hellville to open the 'Tribunal' (Court Building). It has to be said that if the Tribunal building had been situated in any western city, it would undoubtedly have been earmarked for demolition! However, such observations seemed churlish in the face of such obvious pride on the part of the local people. Large gatherings of people, all clothed in colourful 'lamba oanys' (sarongs), took place in various parts of Hellville, and there was much joyful music and singing. Public buildings were decked in flowers and palm fronds and Malgache flags. It was the 'grande fête' and everyone was getting involved and enjoying themselves.

HELLVILLE TO NOSY KOMBA

▼

We headed off for more peaceful waters, just an hour's sail away from Hellville: Nosy Komba. Amidst the most beautiful mountainous scenery, the island of Nosy Komba rises out of the sea, really a complete mountain itself, probably an ancient volcano. On the north-eastern side is the charming village of Ampangorinana, where for the princely sum of R2.50(35 US cents) you can visit the Parc des Lémuriens (the Lemur Park) and have lemurs clamber all over you in search of the bananas which the local children will sell you for R1 (14 US cents) a bunch. It is difficult to know who is more persistent: the lemurs or the children!

When you have tired of the lemurs, you can visit the marvellous beach bar, where you can select anything from the menu as long as it's grilled fish and chips and beer—a bargain at around R60 (US$8.60) for two people. A real feast, delightfully served, but be prepared to wait!

Whilst we were so engaged, downing our THB beers, we chanced to see a young Malgache woman wade into the sea a few yards away. She walked straight in and fell face down in the water. We joked that she was going to drown if she didn't come up for air soon, not realising that anything was amiss. Then suddenly a young man ran down to the water and pulled her out. By this time, a whole crowd of people had gathered, including a European lady who explained to us that the girl had been drinking and had expressed a wish to kill herself. We should have realised that something was wrong, for Malgache women do not go into the sea like that and do not swim. We watched in stunned disbelief as the family hustled the half-drowned girl away to their hut. Nothing more was heard on the matter. Evidently the young lady did not share our view that Nosy Komba is paradise. If you don't have the freedom to do as you please, I guess any place becomes hell after a while.

We were anchored a little way from the main village, in front of a small enclave of buildings known locally as 'Stephano's'. Apparently, Stephano is an Italian doctor who has set up a school here for the local children. Schooling in Madagascar seems to be patchy, mainly due to a lack of teachers. What teachers there are tend to go to private schools and most of the local people cannot afford these. Unfortunately, we did not meet Stephano, but we met several other Europeans who were staying there, some of them volunteering their services for the benefit of the school. The attraction for us was the free availability of good drinking water there, which is piped directly down from the cloud-enveloped heights of Nosy Komba's mountain. It was offered in the same generous spirit that Nature herself uses in dispensing her gifts to humankind.

But perhaps most memorable was the chance encounter with an unusual neighbour in our anchorage: a Russian cruising yacht! Her name was 'Nakhodka', which was also the name of her place of origin, near Vladivostok. Aboard was a charming family: Vassily, Nelly and their teenaged son, Ivan. They had come via Japan, Vietnam, Singapore and the

Indian Ocean and were heading on to South Africa. We took to them immediately and gave them as much information as we could about Richards Bay and Durban. Vassily had been a ship's captain and he and his family had been cruising for some years. At one stage they had lived in Fort Lauderdale, Florida, where Ivan had attended several years of school and had acquired a rather disconcerting American accent. He had also acquired a taste for surfing and could hardly wait to get to Durban to try out the waves there.

We spent a further day at Nosy Komba, catching up on washing, bread-making and socialising with our Russian neighbours. It was a peaceful anchorage in terms of not being pestered by local people, but at night the wind tended to come up, making it quite bouncy and driving in some fairly heavy rain. During the day, pleasant walks were to be had along the beaches or up the mountain, although we declined the latter after Ivan and his mother mentioned they had seen snakes on the path. (I discovered later that Madagascar has no snakes which are dangerous to humans because their fangs are not in the front, but in the backs of their mouths). Ivan had made friends amongst the local youngsters and told us all about a village fete he attended, where the main entertainment had been Malgache boxing, the usual bare-knuckle affair that sounded like a bit of a free-for-all!

We discovered that cruising boats in the Nosy Be area keep in contact on 4417kH on SSB radio at 7am local time in English and 8am in German. It was a good way to glean information. For instance, we found out that the Port Authorities in Hellville hold onto the original papers of visiting yachts and only return them when yachts clear out. Costs for clearing in were US$100 and more. With our 3-month clearance and visas in our passports, we had not felt it necessary to approach the authorities.

Apparently, in previous years, a certain notorious Captain Olivier had been wont to overindulge in the bottle and commandeer a yacht to hunt down unfortunate cruisers who had refused to pay his extortionate demands. In his defence, it has to be said that he was very helpful to a friend of ours who once found himself stranded in Hellville, and well worth the price of a few beers at a local hostelry. In any event, we heard that the excesses of previous years were no longer the norm and there had been no stories of extortion that year. Nevertheless, we steered clear of the authorities on the premise that it is best not to give them the opportunity, and we certainly did not want to hand over original documents!

On 24 July, we hopped back to Hellville briefly to stock up on fresh provisions, saying farewell to 'Nakhodka', who, appropriately, was heading for 'Russian Bay'. We met up with 'Fujimo' again and enjoyed catching up with their news over a braai that night. We tucked into enormous and delicious prawns at R30 (US$4) a kilo from the market, and large pieces of Zebu meat which was tasty but tough, washed down with a cheek-grabbing local wine! That night the heavens opened again, understandably in such a mountainous area, but luckily the rain only started after we were safely aboard our own boat.

Tany Kely And Russian Bay

▼

On 25 July, we sailed the four or five miles south from Hellville to the charming island of Tany Kely. It is a favourite destination of day-trippers and divers, with a beautiful reef close to the shore. Snorkelling revealed huge, colourful parrot fish, square-shaped puffer fish, iridescent damsel fish, dramatic black and white zebra fish, and many more. The fish seemed quite tame as we swam amongst them. Aside from the excellent snorkelling, we were delighted to find a mooring buoy not far from the beach on the east side, which obviated the tiresome work of dropping an anchor. We tied up there for the night and no one said 'boo' to us. The day-trip and diving boats all preferred to get right up to the beach during their brief daytime visits.

At low tide, we took a walk right round Tany Kely. At the north end is a huge, free-standing rock and on the west side are several caves and secret coves. The centre of the island rises quite steeply and is covered by impenetrable jungle. At the highest point stands a disused lighthouse and next to it a rather nice-looking little house with a verandah from which the views must be superb, if it is still occupied. The only human residents we came across seemed to be using a small tent near the beach. One of them was a local man who made intriguing wooden novelties to sell to the tourists, including beautifully-carved hats that one could actually wear! The only other residents we could see were the white, long-tailed tropic birds and multitudes of flying foxes which emerged from their perches in the trees at dusk, whole black clouds of them, flitting and squeaking and hunting insects, no doubt. Through the night we could still hear them and catch glimpses of them by the light of a half-moon. It was a most beautiful and peaceful spot.

Next day, 26 July, we left Tany Kely early for Ambavatoby Bay, better known as Russian Bay, some 13 miles west, on Madagascar itself. We had to motor-sail for most of the way into a light west-north-westerly wind, passing several fishing pirogues which seemed to love paddling like mad directly across our bows: a local variant of the 'chicken game' perhaps? Later, a former ship's officer who had been out in Indonesia, told us that the locals there do exactly the same thing. They believe that this manoeuvre transfers any evil spirits following their vessel onto yours! Since the first inhabitants of Madagascar came from Indonesia, it seems likely that such beliefs were transplanted with them.

We found it rather tricky getting into Russian Bay, as GPS-derived positions did not tally with the elderly charts of the area and if you cut the corner too much on the east side of the entrance, you start getting into some very shallow water. In the end, we found the easiest way of fixing our position was to take compass bearings on the headlands and we soon passed safely through into this magnificent natural harbour. The anchorage is on the west side in front of the tiny settlement of Andassy Be. When approaching the anchorage, one should be mindful of a sandspit which extends about 500m south from the west headland of the Bay, but other than that it is quite straightforward.

Apparently Russian Bay gets its intriguing name from the crew of a Russian warship, the 'Vlotny', which played hookey from the Russo-Japanese War in 1905. They built a large Uralian-style dormitory and other premises at Andassy Be, and survived by fishing, trading and a little piracy until the ship ran out of coke for the boilers! Malaria and other diseases took their toll and apparently the last of the crew died in 1936. While alive, they certainly built well, using solid blocks of stone. One can still see the remains of the dormitory, with what looks like a fort attached, as well as some ruined bridge supports and steps leading up to the site of the commander's house on a hill overlooking the Bay. It is said that the remains of the ship can still be seen at low tide, but all we could make out were the rotting ribs of a vessel that looked more like one of the local 'boutres' than a warship.

It was certainly one of the most beautiful and calm anchorages that we had yet encountered. For company, we had 'Nakhodka', South African yacht 'Con Brio' and a little 26-foot Australian yacht called 'Possibilities'. All the crews got together for a party on 'Nakhodka' that night, everyone contributing food and drinks galore. It was the first time I had tried the local rum and found it very smooth, but powerful stuff, even after considerable dilution with water! It was pleasant to be in the company of other cruising folks again and in such magnificent surroundings. The dramatic mountains all around us were sometimes swathed in cloud and swept by rain squalls. Beneath us, the water was full of turtles and fish, including the occasional jumping manta ray and the slightly sinister-looking sucker fish that hung around under the boat, darting out to gobble any bits of organic waste that we ditched over the side. The presence of these fish did nothing to encourage us to swim off the boat, despite assurances that they were completely harmless.

The little settlement of Andassy Be was extremely poor and primitive, but the locals were pleasant and did their best to offer us things to buy. However, they really had nothing that we wanted! Mangroves grew in abundance in the shallows around the mouth of a dried-up river which divided one group of huts from the other. The mangroves attracted varied bird life, including exquisite, tiny kingfishers hunting for their dinner in the rich waters of the Bay. On a flat area by the river was a sizable coconut plantation and through it various paths led into the jungle beyond. Charming local girls, laughing and chattering, clothed in their lamba oanys, would wade along by the shore trying to catch tiny fish in a net. They were assisted by a little lad and an extremely scruffy old dog, who nevertheless was doing a competent job of scaring up the small fry. We stood and watched this simple and idyllic scene that accorded so well with the peace and quiet of the place.

Later, we did some snorkelling off the reefs at the entrance to the Bay, with some of the folks from 'Nakhodka' and 'Con Brio'. Visibility was not very good, but we could discern a large variety of corals and some big fish, particularly parrot fish. The others tried spearfishing, sadly with little success. To restore our spirits, we all met up that evening on 'Con Brio' for drinks and snacks. It was a lot of fun, as Vassily regaled us with stories of his yacht racing exploits off Vladivostok. It sounded challenging, particularly when he told us they often had to contend with thick fog and that some places up there have as much as a 22-metre range of tide! Who would have thought we would be sitting here in Russian Bay, Madagascar, with some *real* Russians, sharing our sailing experiences? It's a small world indeed!

The Islands Of Ampasindava Bay

▼

On 29 July, we said farewell to our Russian friends and to the folks on 'Con Brio' and headed a little way east of Russian Bay to another large natural harbour called Ampasindava Bay. Lying directly across from Nosy Be and ringed by massive mountain ranges, this scenic bay offers yet more delightful anchorages right in the heart of this popular cruising area. Our first destination was the island of Nosy Kisimany, just inside the Bay on the west side. The anchorage was well-sheltered, off a white coral sand beach. All was well, although the spring tide range of 5 metres was somewhat alarming! Snorkelling revealed a shoal of barracuda and a small blue-spotted ray hiding in solitary splendour under a rock. A local lad paddled up in his fishing pirogue and sold us a big fish for the equivalent of R5 (70 US cents) plus some empty bottles. The white flesh was good eating and provided us with two substantial meals.

Nosy Kisimany lies not far off the Madagascar mainland and consists of two islands linked by a drying sandspit. Opposite our anchorage was a deep indentation in the coastline which would provide a well-protected 'hurricane hole' type of anchorage, although less scenic than the Nosy Kisimany side. All around, as far as the eye could see, were imposing mountains. It was a beautiful spot and to make it even more perfect we were joined by some dolphins, who played around the boat as we enjoyed our sundowners.

Next day, 30 July, we carried on down into Ampasindava Bay to the next cluster of islands, chief of which is Nosy Mamoko. It was a short hop of about 11 miles and, as with Nosy Kisimany, we found a sheltered anchorage between the islands and the nearby shore. If anything, the coastal mountain ranges were even more impressive in this part of the Bay, and thick vegetation covered most of the land. Nosy Mamoko seemed engulfed in a green sea of jungle, its trees smothered by luxuriant waves of creepers. Even the mangroves along the shore seemed to be of several distinct varieties. A tiny village was crammed onto the only area of relatively flat land at one end of the island, most of its huts being built upon stilts. The usual parade of locals came paddling by in their pirogues, trying to sell us things and desperately seeking items such as fishing line, hooks, rope and empty bottles. The latter were really the only things we could spare them.

The anchorage, set in the elbow formed by the main, hilly part of the island and the flat peninsula on which the village stood, was deep but peaceful and secure. We were not alone. A yacht called 'Qu'importe' (roughly translated as 'So What'), registered in Brittany, France, had got there before us. We hardly saw any sign of life on board, except as we were leaving: a middle-aged European with a golden-hued young lady. An interesting mix of cool Breton and warm Malgache, perhaps? Unfortunately, we did not get to know them.

Nosy Mamoko was quite a wildlife paradise. From their jungle fastness, fish eagles filled the air with their sharp cries. We saw herons in abundance and the locals told us there were turtles and 'maki' (lemur) about. As for fish, many times we saw shoals ruffling the surface of the water, but we had no luck when it came to catching any of them! No fish, but pleasant memories of another lovely anchorage.

CRATER BAY, NOSY BE

On 31 July, we left Nosy Mamoko and Ampasindava Bay for Crater Bay (Anse du Cratère)on the island of Nosy Be, just across the water. Leaving early, we reached Crater Bay by mid-afternoon. This popular anchorage is a short distance to the west of Hellville, and when we arrived we found it packed with yachts, charter boats and fishing craft, some of which were on permanent chain moorings. In addition to these hazards, there were some sneaky rocks and shoaling patches around, so it was very difficult to find a suitable spot to anchor. Australian yacht 'Possibilities' had found a nice secure spot, but we were not so lucky. During the first night there we dragged and next morning found ourselves just about on top of a very fancy big yacht flying an Italian flag. The crewman on board was very helpful, even diving to see if our anchor chain was fouled on his or on some other obstruction. Fortunately all was well and the chain had simply taken a few dog-legs around some rocks on the sea bed. We upped anchor and moved well away but it took several tries, and near-exhaustion for poor Don, before we got the anchor to hold securely.

After that excitement, we went ashore in the dinghy and found that the boat boys/gardiens were more pleasant and less pushy than in Hellville. We soon found a taxi, whose driver, Bernard, took us to Hellville by a cir-cuitous route which took us through the neighbouring settlement of Ambatoloaka, to the west of the extinct volcano which gives Crater Bay its name. Ambatoloaka was a revelation: a lively place, full of Malgache huts, shops and restaurants cheek by jowl with European-style hotels and resorts fronting a sweep of sandy bay. Busy with locals and tourists alike, it exuded a happy and relaxed atmosphere. It was here that Bernard had us transfer to a marginally less ancient vehicle; one in which we were not entertained by a view of the road rushing by under our feet as we drove along! Bernard conducted us safely around our provisioning stops in Hellville and back to Crater Bay in one piece, so we asked him to take us the next day on a tour of Nosy Be. The price agreed was R200 (US$29) for both of us (half the going rate for organised tours).

Bright and early next morning, we set off with Bernard on our tour. The first stop was the perfume distillery set among the hills above Hellville, where fragrant ylang-ylang blossoms are transformed into essences, which are exported to France to be used as the basis of expensive perfumes. All around us stretched acres of ylang-ylang trees, their tops pollarded to enable the flower-pickers to reach the blossoms. The leaves are set in serried ranks on either side of the long branches. The flowers have an exquisite scent, not unlike jasmine, but are unattractive, being pale yellow and rather straggly. Apparently harvesting goes on throughout the year and provides employment to some of the local people. Stopping to examine the trees more closely, we saw several weird and brightly coloured chameleons clinging to the branches. Apparently their colours are influenced by their moods, so some of these chaps were either very angry or just showing off to their pals! Among these hills, Bernard also pointed out to us coffee and citronella plants growing wild. We found citronella oil most effective as a mosquito repellent.

Then we headed over to the west coast of Nosy Be, to the town of Dzamandzar, famous for the distilling of quite a different commodity: rum! The distillery is set amongst huge tracts of sugar cane, criss-crossed by dirt roads on which heavy loads of cut cane trundle in to be processed. Security at the distillery compound was tight and, unfortunately, no tours were scheduled for that day. We had to content ourselves with the exterior view of the massive complex and with the purchase of a dark and lethal-looking brew from the gate-man. For R25 (US$3.60) he filled our 1-litre plastic bottle with rum straight from the distillery. It was powerful stuff, even after dilution with water, and the bluish tinge of the plastic made it look strangely like methylated spirits! We drank it and survived to tell the tale, anyway.

We carried on up the west coast to a prominent headland called Pointe d'Andilah. Beside it we found a lovely white sandy bay, fringed by reefs and complemented by a picturesque off-lying island. Behind the beach, several resort hotels were set amongst palm groves, some blending in better than others. Despite the size of the hotels, the beach was uncrowded and we enjoyed a quiet, shady spot under a palm tree, while locals plied us very courteously with souvenirs and fresh coconuts. As we consumed the milk and flesh of the coconuts, a gentle Malgache girl, her face painted with intricate designs, offered us a massage. Not knowing quite what to expect, we declined.

Soon it was time for lunch and we made our way up from the beach to a little Malgache restaurant, owned by a large, ebullient fellow called Ernest, who seemed to be a pal of Bernard's. We had superb, freshly caught lobster and fish, with coconut-flavoured rice. However, when the meal was over, we got a shock when we were presented with a bill for R240 (US$34), which did not bear any resemblance to the menu prices! After remonstrating with Ernest, we got R60 (US$8.60) taken off the bill, but it seemed pretty obvious that he had been 'trying it on' with us. Needless to say, the atmosphere after that was somewhat strained.

As with all these local restaurants, the toilet facilities left much to be desired. In this case, they took the form of a bare shed with an earth floor on which a wooden plank had been laid to walk on. As I entered, I noticed that the earth floor contained several holes, into which scuttled some sizable crabs! It was disconcerting, to say the least, to be sharing a 'loo' with these creatures. However, I was mightily relieved to find that crab was *not* on the menu of the establishment.

The final stop on our tour was Mont Passot (Pic du Tanilatsaka), one of the highest points on Nosy Be, from whose summit we enjoyed a breathtaking view covering a radius of a good 30 miles or more. Mountains, bays and islands spread before us, from Nosy Iranja in the south-west right up to the Mitsio Islands in the north-east. At our feet was the island of Sakatia, lying just off the west coast of Nosy Be. Around us were lakes which had formed in the craters of extinct volcanoes and which were said to contain crocodiles. The descent from Mont Passot was very exciting, following a dirt track which looked as though it had been gouged out of the mountainside by flood waters. At times it seemed only a 4x4 vehicle could have got through, but our valiant little taxi made it, much to our surprise, and delivered us safely back to Crater Bay. We settled up with Bernard, but he did not get any gratuities or 'presents', as the restaurant rip-off still rankled.

SAKATIA ISLAND

On 3 August, we departed Crater Bay in the company of a school of friendly dolphins and motor-sailed the 8 miles or so around to Sakatia Island on the west side of Nosy Be. There we dropped anchor in front of Sakatia Passions, a game fishing resort nestling in a sheltered cove on the east side of the little island. Sharing the anchorage was American-registered yacht 'Cloud Seven', with Richard and Krista aboard. They had been cruising since 1992 and their next destinations were Mayotte and Durban. Together we enjoyed this secluded spot, with views across to the Nosy Be mountains on one side and to hilly and rock-fringed Sakatia on the other.

Ashore we found areas of lush tropical vegetation, including the beautiful fan-shaped ravinala or traveller's palm, so named because a thirsty traveller can always find refreshing rainwater trapped amongst the thick leaf-bases. There were also tall kapok trees, with their long sausage-shaped pods bursting with a cotton-like material. Coconut palms and coral trees also grew in abundance. We explored a jungle path up behind Sakatia Passions lodge, which brought us out onto a pleasant view-site on a small hill, before plunging down again into dense forest and eventually arriving in the next cove, which was home to a community of Malgache fishermen. We returned via the coastal walk, which turned into a strenuous and exciting scramble over weird and wonderful sea-sculpted rocks. We were glad to get back and relax in the comfortable lounge bar at Sakatia Passions lodge. Out of curiosity we enquired about their accommodation rates and found them considerably cheaper than the Nosy Iranja resort, at around R350 (US$50) per person per night, plus transfers to the island of about R150 (US$21).

At the south-eastern corner of the island is a South African-owned scuba diving resort called Sakatia Dive Inn. We contacted them on VHF Channel 9 and arranged to go diving the following day. The cost was R200 (US$29) each, including hire of equipment. Our instructor was a very calm and competent Frenchman called Stefan, who picked us up from our yacht and took us out to a nearby reef called Olaf Bank, with a maximum depth of 16 metres. We explored amongst colourful corals of all shapes and sizes, inhabited by giant clams, ugly crocodile fish, flamboyant lion fish, graceful butterfly fish and a host of others. Suddenly Stefan pointed above us to a dark, menacing shape which I was sure was a shark but which turned out to be a large barracuda. All too soon our time was up and we were picked up by the dive boat and deposited at Sakatia Dive Inn for showers and a complimentary beer. It had been a most enjoyable afternoon.

MITSIO ISLANDS

―――――――▼―――――――

On 5 August, we set off for the Mitsio Islands, which lie to the north-east of Nosy Be. We broke our journey at Mahazandri Bay on the east coast of Nosy Be, which proved to be a rather bouncy anchorage in the prevailing easterly swells. Next day we crossed to the Mitsio Islands, passing close to the impressive basalt monoliths known as The Four Brothers (Les Quatres Frères). A favourite trick of people on passing boats seems to be to clap their hands to make the multitude of seabirds take off like a great white cloud from the rocks. Our course took us around the west side of the largest of the Mitsio Islands and into the recommended anchorage of Maribe Bay.

Up until then we had had no luck with our fishing, despite passing leaping bonito shoals, pursued by eager dolphins. As we came into Maribe Bay, I glanced behind us and saw a great thrashing in the water. We hauled in the line to find a magnificent 10-15lb game fish called a 'wahoo' snared with a piece of silver paper as bait! Throughout our cruise, we found the fancy lures and 'rubber squid' to be a dead loss (we imagined the fish saying: 'Rubbair squeed, wat ees zis rubbair squeed? I speet on your rubbair squeed'), but pieces of bread, plastic or silver paper turned out to be a hit! Our wahoo was superb eating, fried in butter and lemon juice. In fact there was so much that we gave some away to our neighbours in the anchorage, a pleasant French couple, who were delighted with the unexpected gift.

Contrary to all appearances, Maribe Bay was quite a rolly anchorage when the swells swept in from the north. However, some rain made for a pleasantly cool night and we awoke well-rested the next morning. We went ashore in the dinghy and disposed of our refuse by burning and then burying it on the beach, an act which attracted curious onlookers from the nearby village. Due to the presence of cattle on Nosy Mitsio, large tracts of land are under savannah grassland rather than forest and it was easy to climb the well-worn tracks to the top of a nearby hill. From there the views were magnificent.

High above us four fish eagles soared and squabbled in the air. We watched spellbound as two of them grasped each other by the talons and went spiralling downwards as if to dash each other to pieces on the ground beneath. At the last moment they disengaged from each other and swooped off in different directions like members of an aerobatic team. It was an incredible show!

We made our way back to the beach, past clumps of fan-palms and a group of huge, ancient mango trees, whose vast network of gnarled, inter-twined roots completely covered the ground beneath them. Later we explored Maribe Bay in the dinghy. While egrets and gannets swooped in the air above us, a huge manta ray (about 4 feet across) leaped out of the water right beside us. The coral reefs around the edges of the bay were clearly visible through the clear water. It was an unspoiled and very beau-tiful place.

After another rather rolly and rainy night, we moved across to a strik-ing, square-shaped volcanic island called Nosy Ankarea, about 3 miles off the north-west coast of Nosy Mitsio. Surrounded by perfect white coral sand, the black basalt rock of Nosy Ankarea rose dramatically straight out of the sea. There we found some of the best snorkelling yet, in very clear water. For the first time, I was able to get close to two hawksbill turtles, one small and the other large. The latter was quite unaware of my presence, hovering near the bottom and gazing intently at a clump of coral. I dived down to get a closer look and he took off in fright, flapping his fin-like legs faster and faster like a bird trying to take off! I didn't even try to keep up with him. As well as the turtles, there was a variety of fish, including large parrot fish, and there were giant clams and many colourful corals. On shore, we discovered an exquisite bush camp resort, owned by the Marlin Club of Nosy Be and run by a charming lady called Francesca, who gave us a warm welcome. Visiting yachts are free to make use of the resort's mooring buoys, situated just off the beach.

After a sociable reunion with our new French friends with whom we had shared our fish, we left Nosy Ankarea and returned to the west side of Nosy Mitsio, where we anchored just off a sweep of deserted sandy beach. Ashore, we took a long walk on the golden, pristine sands, lapped by gentle waves, and enjoyed a dramatic sunset which made the great square lump of rock that is Nosy Ankarea look eerily like something from 'Close Encounters of the Third Kind'!

On 9 August, we left Nosy Mitsio, motor-sailing around its northern extremity and down its eastern side. We made a lunch stop at another of the Mitsio Islands, Tsara Bajina, lying to the south of Nosy Mitsio and looking like a desert island created by Walt Disney! It had everything: white sand, palms, rocks, beautiful coral reefs and fish galore.

Despite what is said in the pilot book, yachts can now only anchor on its north-western side, as the south side is reserved for the seaplane which serves a fancy new resort there. As we left Tsara Bajina, we watched the seaplane taking off and got quite a thrill when it buzzed us. It did it again later and just about scared the pants off us with the sudden blast of noise from the engines. It had crept up on us unawares, from behind, skimming just a few feet above the sea! While the seaplane arrived back in Nosy Be in no time, it took us from early afternoon until after dark to reach Mahazandri Bay, on the east side of Nosy Be, once again.

Clearing Out Of Nosy Be

▼

We were very grateful for radar as we made our way into Mahazandri Bay, on the east side of Nosy Be, after dark on 9 August. We anchored in almost the same spot as before, but this time without wind or swell it was a most peaceful place. Next day, 10 August, was our 27th wedding anniversary as well as the birthday of our dear friend, Sally, cruising aboard the yacht 'Dawn' up on the East African coast. We thanked our lucky stars for our robust health when we learned that 'Dawn's' owner, Woody, was slowly recovering from a nasty bout of malaria.

We spent the day in not very romantic fashion, motor-sailing to Nosy Komba to do our washing and take on the fresh water which runs all the way to the village from the mountain-top lake. Next day, we made our way across to Hellville to take on fuel, gas and provisions and to clear out for Mayotte. We made good progress with the various chores, although shopping in Hellville can take about ten years off your life, it's such a madhouse!

We enjoyed a belated anniversary dinner that night at a charming French restaurant in town, called 'Le Papillon', which seems to have dropped out of favour these days, in the face of newer and trendier competitors. However, we had no complaints with the meal at a total of R145 (US$21), which included a superb home-made ice-cream, delicately flavoured with locally-grown vanilla pods. As we strolled through

Hellville's main street that evening, we found an excellent boat supply shop called 'MegaBe'. There we chatted to the pleasant staff and ended up buying a beautifully-carved wooden paddle, to replace the one we had lost in the surf at Nosy Iranja. The staff proudly told us it was the product of a scheme they had going to keep the local youngsters off the streets. Well, we certainly weren't complaining at R35 (US$5) for a solid hardwood paddle!

Next day was Saturday, 12 August, and we presented ourselves and our passports at Hellville police station for clearance to proceed to our next destination, which was to be Mayotte, the French island set in the middle of the Mozambique Channel, a couple of days' sail away. During our time in the Nosy Be area we had not troubled the Port Captain's office and they had not troubled us, and that day was no exception. Besides, the Port Captain's office was closed over the weekend! The gentleman who looked after immigration matters at the police station was only too delighted to stamp our passports in return for the princely sum of R35 (US$5), which he cheerfully conceded was going straight into his back pocket! (We found that as long as our passports were in order, the Port Captain's office in Mayotte was not overly concerned about seeing any clearance documents from the Port Captain of Hellville.)

Thirsty after our exertions at immigration and in purchasing some last minute provisions, we adjourned to the popular Oasis Bar in the centre of town, and who should we meet but Graham and Veronica from Durban-registered catamaran 'Arran' , together with the owner of Sakatia Dive Inn, Jose. (Little did we know it, but some weeks later, while Graham and Veronica were in Mayotte, their yacht was to be almost destroyed by fire, probably caused by an electrical fault. Fortunately, they were not on board at the time, but most of their possessions were lost, despite prompt and courageous action by French Navy firefighters and neighbouring yachts-people.) After much catching up on news and gossip, they persuaded us to make a rendezvous at Russian Bay two days hence for a birthday celebration for a youngster from one of the American cruising boats. We made our way there via the beautiful, reef-fringed island of Tany Kely and on 14 August we found ourselves anchored amidst a crowd of over a dozen cruising and charter boats in the huge natural harbour of Russian Bay.

The South African boats, besides ours, were 'Arran' (Graham & Veronica, Durban), 'Con Brio' (Gerard & Anita, Simonstown), 'Kinda Magic' (Charles & Marian, East London), and little 'Catch 22' from Richards Bay. The Australian yachts were 'Yawarra' (Nick & Jan) and 'Possibilities' (Jamie & Laura). Sole New Zealand yacht was 'Erasmus' (Craig & Mary). The American yachts were 'Chandelle', whose owner Bob had crewed on 'Gone With The Wind' when she was being taken through the Panama Canal by her previous owner (small world!); and 'Beau Soleil' with Mike, Karen and, most importantly, Falcon their son, whose 12th birthday we were all there to celebrate.

There was a big beach party, with a fish braai and pot luck contributions to the groaning buffet table from each yacht. When it came time for beach sports, it was a case of South Africa versus The Rest of The World. The tug o' war ended in a one all draw and the water-volleyball engendered such hilarity that we all lost count of the score! It was a lovely day, full of fun and good fellowship, and rounded off by a very noisy firework display organised by Falcon and some of the other cruising youngsters. A birthday to remember.

With some regret, we realised our time in Madagascar was coming to an end. Mayotte beckoned and we would set sail next day, 15 August, leaving behind the good friends we had made, the wild mountain scenery, the dramatic cloudscapes bringing refreshing night-time rains, the playful dolphins, and acrobatic fish leaping high into the air and occasionally landing in the cockpit of some lucky yacht! Our cruising had barely scratched the surface of Madagascar, yet we would take away with us so many impressions and memories of this strange and fascinating land, a land full of enticements to further exploration.

As with any 'frontier land', such exploration is not without risk. The cruising sailor must always be vigilant when navigating or anchoring in

Malagasy waters, as available charts are old and none too reliable. That same year an unfortunate South African cruising couple lost their yacht when it dragged its anchor and wrecked itself on a beach in the south-west of Madagascar. Another risk is that of theft, particularly of outboard engines, always a temptation in a land where the people have so very little. We always hoisted our rubber dinghy aboard at night and kept our outboard engine secured with a padlock and never had any trouble.

As to personal safety, we never felt threatened, particularly amongst the gentle people of the villages. We had heard stories about Majunga, so we always fitted our burglar bars at night there. We were not aware of anyone even attempting to board us, unlike one single-hander that same year who anchored at Majunga and went to sleep leaving all his hatches open. He awoke to find several jovial young men on his boat, who amidst much laughing and joking, proceeded to tie him up, beat him and demand money and handguns! It has to be said that during our time in Madagascar this was the only incident of violent crime against a cruising yachtsman we heard of (apart from the notorious Nosy Lava incident some years back), and hopefully it was an isolated aberration.

A more insidious threat is that of disease. Precautions against malaria and cholera should be taken seriously and a comprehensive medical kit, including antibiotics, should be carried. Occasionally, we heard of yachtsmen taking pity on villagers and dishing out antibiotics for various complaints. The most serious difficulty with this is that, without adequate supervision, the patient often stops taking the drugs as soon as he or she begins to feel better, so aiding the development of drug-resistant strains of bacteria. That is assuming the antibiotics even reach the patient, for the temptation is always there for the very poor to sell or trade them on for more basic necessities. In the end, well-meaning people are doing more harm than good.

As to the costs involved in cruising Madagascar, we found we could live very comfortably on US$400-500 per month, including water, fuel, port charges, food and drinks. Before we left, we stocked up in South Africa with plenty of canned goods, dried milk powder, tea and coffee, instant soups and sauces, paper towels, sweets and all the other First World luxury items that are unobtainable in Madagascar. If you can supplement your diet by catching fish, so much the better. Items such as rice, dried beans, popcorn, fish, seafood, a limited variety of fruit and vegetables, Zebu meat, and in some places spices and honey, can be bought fairly cheaply in the markets. Packaged foodstuffs from South Africa and France are available in the larger centres, but tend to be quite expensive. We also took vitamin and mineral supplements and remained healthy throughout our trip. In fact, after all the exercise and abstinence from goodies such as ice-cream, we were both considerably lighter and fitter than when we left. On our return to 'civilisation', we laughed at all the advertisements for 'fad' diets. No need for any of those—just go sailing!

To anyone contemplating cruising the coasts of Madagascar I would say: yes, go now while they are still primitive and unspoiled, for sadly they cannot remain so indefinitely. Be sensible and you will enjoy a happy and healthy time. It is an experience you will never forget!

EPILOGUE

Perhaps some of you may be curious to learn what became of us after we left Madagascar and how we fared on the voyage back to South Africa. Well, we set off for the French island of Mayotte on 15 August, 2000, and had an uneventful 2½-day passage to this mountainous and scenic island, which sits in the middle of the Mozambique Channel between Madagascar and Africa. It is surrounded by a barrier reef, beautiful but deadly to the unwary seafarer, through which one has to pass to enter the lagoon. We chose to enter through the Passe Bandélé, on the south-east side, and were swept in with the incoming tide, surrounded by dolphins and pirogues hunting for fish in the foamy blue-green waters, while on either hand breakers crashed in long lines upon the reefs as far as the eye could see. Once through the reef, it took us about 2 hours to reach the main port and anchorage of Dzaoudzi, situated on a small island lying just off the north-east coast of Mayotte.

As soon as we made contact with the Port Captain, we knew we were back in 'civilisation' again! Bureaucracy was minimal and free of charge. It was pleasant to be able to go about one's business without being assailed for handouts at every turn. We made friends with yachtspeople of many nationalities who were stopping over there and we did quite a bit of exploring and snorkelling. We enjoyed it so much, we stayed for a month!

The cost of living was much higher than in Madagascar, but things were efficiently run and there was such a variety of produce in the shops and open-air markets. There was even an Internet café! Much development was taking place, so that, although the villages were perhaps not as picturesque as those of Madagascar, at least the people were getting roofs over their heads, basic sanitation, water and electricity.

Mayotte voted some years ago to remain a French territory, while its geographical neighbours, the Comores Islands opted to form a Muslim Republic. However, one of the Comores, Anjouan, has been the scene of recent political unrest because it seems they also want to enjoy the manifold benefits of being a French territory once again! Consequently, many Anjouan people attempt to get into Mayotte, some risking their lives by crossing the sea in flimsy craft. It would have been interesting to see the Comores, but while we were in Mayotte we heard there were riots going on there, so we gave them a miss.

In mid-September we finally dragged ourselves away from the First World comforts and delicious French delicacies of Mayotte. It took us 3½ days to sail to the African mainland, carried on south-westerly to south-easterly winds and a variety of currents and counter currents in the Mozambique Channel. During the trip, delightful speckled dolphins would sometimes join us at dusk and dawn, joyfully leaping from the water all around us. At night, seabirds would swoop and call. For 2 nights running, a gannet used our boat as a resting place, perching either on the tail of our wind-generator or on the top of the mast, where it remained, glaring down at us for most of the night!

Our first port of call was Pemba (Porto Amelia) in the far north of Mozambique. We had hoped to venture further north to Kenya and Tanzania, but the prevailing winds and currents would have been against us at that time of year for the return journey to South Africa. There was no doubt about it, Mozambique was impressive. Once classed as the poorest country in the world, ravaged by war and periodic flooding, it was now pulling itself up by its bootstraps, with the aid of massive foreign investment and sheer hard work.

We liked Pemba. Set on a magnificent hill site, it enjoyed commanding views both out to sea and inland over a vast lake surrounded by rolling, scrubby terrain. Although in a similar condition to the ports we had seen in Madagascar, there seemed to be a greater air of optimism about. A new harbour had been built; repairs were being done to roads and services; the little houses were being painted and flower gardens were blooming around them; the children could be seen going off to school in neat uniforms. Communicating with people was limited, for we spoke minimal Portuguese and very few of them spoke English, but all were invariably friendly towards us. Sitting at anchor in the bay below the town, we enjoyed a daily chorus of the Muslim call to prayer from a nearby mosque and the melodious singing of squads of fishermen rowing by in their boats.

As in Madagascar, the bureaucracy was convoluted. The Port Captain charged us US$30 for unlimited stops at ports throughout Mozambique. Immigration charged us US$55 each for 1-month multi-entry visas, plus a small 'border tax', and they even charged us for the forms we had to fill in! However, once the formalities were out of the way, we could relax and stroll around the town. We knew we were back in Africa again. The air was filled with birdsong; the joyful shouts of kids playing football on the beach; the fragrance of blossoming trees; the acrid smell of wood smoke and cattle. We visited a marvellous traditional boatyard where beautiful wooden fishing trawlers (traineiras) were being constructed under the direction of a Portuguese gentleman who was the last of a long line of wooden boat-builders. He even carried his lineage with him in his surname 'Calafato', which means 'caulker'.

We took a long walk towards the sea, passing defaced monuments, derelict military structures and signposts announcing an orphanage and the headquarters of a landmine-clearing organisation. Once past these reminders of the devastating civil war years, we came upon a magnificent sweep of white sand, with reefs and green algae-covered rocks, emerald water and fishing boats galore. Wandering on, we passed the neat bungalows abandoned by the Portuguese and now inhabited by the locals, and soon found ourselves in the fishermen's quarter of palm-thatched, daub and wattle huts. People greeted us and one enterprising lady invited us into her 'shebeen', where we enjoyed refreshments with some of the locals. The shebeen owner's children served drinks, while a charming young girl who spoke a little English chatted to us as she did the ironing.

As in Madagascar, the youngsters were desperate for books, particularly dictionaries, for libraries and bookshops seemed to be as rare as hens' teeth. It was unfortunate that we were unable to help, but if we return I shall certainly take along reading materials for those children. After leaving the shebeen, we passed an immense fallen baobab tree, almost blocking the dusty street, and then came upon a burst main around which children were collecting muddy water in buckets. The beach was full of fishing activity and the business of mending nets. In spite of the evident poverty, people seemed to be busy just getting on with their lives and we were very seldom pestered by beggars.

After a few days, we set sail from Pemba, heading south to explore more of the Mozambique coast. As we left, a large whale breached the sea's surface to bid us farewell, then fell back into the deep, in a colossal white plume of spray. We were aiming for the historic settlement of Ilha de Moçambique, but the weather and the seas did not treat us too kindly, so we headed in to the sheltered bay of the port of Nacala. We stayed only long enough to rest and wait for the weather to improve.

Although the surrounding country was attractive, with odd-shaped volcanic hills and beautiful sandy coves, the town itself was an untidy mixture of high-rise blocks and traditional huts and there was an ugly cement factory on the outskirts. Locals paddled out trying to sell us shells and begging such things as cigarettes, but we got the uneasy feeling they were 'casing the joint'. It was the first time we had ever felt remotely threatened, but we made sure we put our 2hp outboard engine for the dinghy below decks and locked ourselves behind our burglar bars that night, and all was well!

Perhaps another reason for our malaise in Nacala was Don's discovery of an abscess on one of his front teeth! It was an unfortunate situation for anyone to find himself in, particularly a dentist. He was able to keep the infection under control with antibiotics from our extensive medical kit, but of course it meant that our voyage would have to be somewhat curtailed. Don was, understandably, anxious to return to South Africa as soon as possible, where First World standards of healthcare were assured. It was at Nacala too that we heard of the dreadful fire which almost destroyed the cruising catamaran 'Arran' in Mayotte. The airwaves were busy with emotional messages being passed between friends of the owners, a couple from Durban, with whom we had spent such happy times in Madagascar.

We were all very upset at the news. Apparently the owners had been sitting having tea on a neighbouring boat in the Dzaoudzi anchorage. They got to talking about yacht insurance and how so many boats are not covered because of the expense involved. Just then they looked across to their boat and saw that it was on fire! It was fortunate that no-one was on board the yacht at the time of the horrific blaze. By all accounts, the French Navy firefighters were magnificent, responding quickly to the emergency, and many brave yachtspeople pitched in and tried to salvage as much as they could from the yacht before they were beaten back by the flames. We all felt for the owners, who lost so much of their personal belongings and all the mementos one tends to collect over the years. In the true spirit of seafaring folk, the couple were immediately inundated with offers to stay on other boats and ashore with local people, while they tried to salvage what was left of their yacht and make plans to get it back to South Africa. There can be few things more terrifying than fire on a yacht. It was said this one could have been started by an electrical fault. No doubt many a yachtsman was checking his electrical system after that day, and praying it was something that would never happen to him.

Soon we set sail from Nacala and once again received a rousing send-off by the denizens of the deep. This time a whole pod of whales accompanied us through the bay, showing off their manoeuvres: spouting, breaching, tail slapping and generally having a whale of a time! With Don's tooth problem, we had to forego visits to Ilha de Moçambique, Quelimane, Bazaruto Island and Vilanculos. We sailed non-stop to the capital and main port of Maputo (formerly Lourenço Marques), passing the mouth of the mighty Zambezi River and, further south, the famous port of Beira.

We tried to imagine what it must have been like for the inhabitants in the interior, along the banks of Mozambique's great rivers, during the recent floods. Images of a handful of courageous South African helicopter pilots desperately trying to rescue those multitudes of people from the rising waters were still fresh in our memories. How could anyone ever forget the incredible story of the rescue of a young mother and her baby from a tree top, where the baby had just been born! Miraculously, they both survived.

Situated in the far south of Mozambique, Maputo lies on the far side of an immense natural harbour, across which one must navigate to reach the port. As we entered the great bay, masses of dolphins homed in on us, eager to surf our bow wave. I saw 6 or 8 of them on one side alone, swimming in a perfect line-abreast formation, with the sunlight sparkling off their smooth skins as they broke the surface in unison. What a welcome! Maputo itself was a welcoming and impressive city. An amazing amount of development was going on: new harbours, houses, shops, offices and hotels were under construction and a real effort was being made to repair damaged roads.

We tied up in the small craft harbour, where the rotting hulks of some half-submerged naval vessels still remained from the war years. Passage through port formalities was fairly painless, and we were soon strolling the wide boulevards, enjoying the bustle and cosmopolitan atmosphere. Busy cinemas, restaurants and pavement cafés all attested to a joyous return to normality. People were pleasant and helpful. We heard that Portuguese and South African business people were returning in numbers, bringing much-needed investment into the country. White farmers too were being welcomed into the hinterland, particularly the ones now finding themselves kicked out of Zimbabwe! It was a place I really took to, so much so, that I made up my mind to learn Portuguese—for the next time we visit! Being able to communicate with the locals adds so much enjoyment to travelling. I certainly found my French invaluable in Madagascar and Mayotte.

After seeing the sights and doing a bit of re-provisioning, we set off across the bay for a brief sojourn at the lovely island of Inhaca. For company we had South African yacht 'Kinda Magic', also heading home after a cruise to Madagascar. As we both cleared the bay and set sail for South Africa, yet another whale popped up to say 'goodbye'. It came up very close to 'Kinda Magic' and gave the crew quite a thrill. They reckoned they could hear its song reverberating through the steel hull of their boat.

Our first port of call back in South Africa was Richards Bay, where we had quite a reunion with most of the yachtspeople we had met in Madagascar and Mayotte. There were about 10 different nationalities of people there, and one evening we filled a local restaurant and had quite a party. All too soon, it was time to get back to Durban. This final leg of our voyage proved to be the roughest and most exciting. With the strong south-flowing Agulhas Current beneath us and a 40-knot north-easterly gale at our back, building big seas, we had a wild roller-coaster ride down the coast. With just a handkerchief of sail up, we covered the 85 miles from Richards Bay to Durban in 13 hours, which for a 31-foot cruising boat is going some! Approaching Durban, we got drenched when we took a couple of big waves over us. Then it was a case of 'hold onto your hat and don't look back' as we rode the enormous swells right in through the harbour entrance.

We arrived back on 13 October, 2000, safe and sound—apart from Don's tooth! Our yacht 'Gone With The Wind' had behaved like a star throughout our four months and over 6000 miles of voyaging and had never let us down. Now it was time to repay her with a little tender care and get her and ourselves back into condition for the next big adventure. What form will that take? Who knows, and frankly, my dear, I don't give a damn, but whatever it is it will sure beat working!

About the Author

Avril Sellars (née Kelly) was born in 1949 in Edinburgh, Scotland. After achieving her M. A. Honours (French and English Language) from the University of Edinburgh and a Postgraduate Diploma in European Marketing and Languages from the Edinburgh College of Commerce, she worked in government service and later in local government in Scotland. In 1983, she emigrated to Durban, South Africa, with her husband Don (B.D.S. Edinburgh), where she helped him establish a successful dental practice.

It was in South Africa that Avril and Don developed their passion for sailing, logging many thousands of sea miles in races and cruises around the coasts, and completing longer passages across the Indian and Atlantic Oceans. Avril holds the Cruising Association of South Africa Yachtmaster Ocean Certificate as well as the South African D.O.T. Yachtmaster Unlimited Commercial ticket. She was a founder member and past chairman of the South African Ladies' Sailing Association.

Avril has had various articles published in the South African yachting press, the latest being an account of the voyage of 'Gone With The Wind' to Madagascar, which appeared in the February and March, 2001, editions of the 'South African Sailing Magazine'. She and Don live aboard their 11-year-old South African-designed Morganocean 31 'Gone With The Wind', and when not cruising are based in Durban.

Appendix

I BACKGROUND ON MADAGASCAR

Madagascar lies in the south-western Indian Ocean, between 300 and 600 miles off the east coast of Africa. With a total area of over 587000 sq kms (over 226000 sq miles) and a coastline of 4828 kms (3018 miles), it is the world's fourth-largest island. It's climate is tropical along the coast, temperate inland and arid in the south. Tropical cyclones are a hazard, particularly from December to April. A narrow coastal plain rises to a high plateau with mountains in the centre, the highest of which is Maromokotro at 2876 m (9468 ft), situated in northern Madagascar.

Agriculture, fishing and forestry are the mainstay of the economy. Rice is the staple food crop, with coffee and vanilla important cash crops. Cloves, sugar, coconuts, tropical fruits, cotton, sisal and cattle are also farmed. The main industries are meat processing, soap, breweries, tanneries, sugar, textiles, glassware, cement, automobile assembly, paper, petroleum and tourism.

The original inhabitants of Madagascar only arrived on the island about 1500 years ago from Indonesia, possibly via Africa. Collectively known as Malagasy (or in French 'Malgache'), they can be divided into the following ethnic groups:- Malayo-Indonesian, Côtiers (of mixed African, Malayo-Indonesian and Arab ancestry), French, Indian, Creole and Comorian. The total population is estimated at over 15.5 million,

45% of which is under 15 years of age. Annual population growth is estimated at 3%, with a life expectancy of only 55 years.

Madagascar was an independent kingdom until 1896, when it became a French colony. Independence was again established in 1960, under Social Democrat President Philibert Tsiranana. However, his government was seen to be authoritarian, overly pro-French and unable to halt economic decline. Civil unrest led to a suspension of all political parties and the take-over by Admiral Didier Ratsiraka as Head of State and Chairman of the Supreme Revolutionary Council in 1975. His socialist state became known as the Democratic Republic of Madagascar.

Throughout the 1980s, continuing economic hardship and food shortages led to further civil unrest. By the early 1990s, the government permitted the resumption of multi-party politics, abolished press censorship and allowed the establishment of private broadcasting stations. Constitutional amendments were demanded, involving violent clashes with government forces, strikes and an attempted coup. Finally, in 1992 a new constitution was adopted, free elections were held and Albert Zafy served as President from 1992 to 1997. Then in 1997 Didier Ratsiraka was re-elected President and in 1998 a referendum approved new amendments to the constitution, ensuring a federal-style state with a bicameral legislature of Senate and National Assembly.

The President is elected for a 5-year term and can be re-elected for a further two terms. He is responsible for the appointment of a Prime Minister. Classed as a non-aligned country, Madagascar formerly had close links with the Communist block, particularly China, North Korea and the former USSR. President Zafy established relations with South Africa, Israel and South Korea.

France continues to play an important part in the life of Madagascar, being its main trading partner and aid-supplier, in spite of continuing disputes over compensation for nationalised French assets and ownership of certain off-lying islands. The current government seems favourably disposed towards economic reforms and the privatisation of the banking and industrial sectors. The capital is Antananarivo and the official languages are Malagasy and French. Very little English is spoken, except in the most popular tourist areas.

As a 'developing' nation, Madagascar faces the usual problems of malnutrition, lack of health and education funding, a high birth-rate with a low industrial output, soil erosion due to deforestation and overgrazing, contamination of surface water and the endangerment of several unique species of flora and fauna. The growth of the economy has been hampered by anti-government strikes and demonstrations, a decline in world coffee demand and a lack of economic reform. The government will have to address these problems, as well as attract foreign investment, if the country's full potential is to be realised. An estimated economic growth rate of 5% has been suggested for the year 2000-2001.

Madagascar's varied topography, climatic zones and isolation have made it one of Nature's treasure-houses. It is home not only to the famous lemurs but also to two-thirds of the world's chameleons and to many other unique species of reptiles, birds, insects and plants. It bore witness to some extraordinary creatures which are now extinct, such as the giant tortoise, the pygmy hippo and the Aepiornis (Elephant Bird) which stood 10 feet tall, weighed about 200 lbs and, not surprisingly, was classed as the largest bird in the world. There are still some pretty extraordinary creatures which continue to exist in Madagascar, principally the aye-aye, a mammal with bat ears, rodent teeth and a bony middle finger for extricating insects from crevices in trees. There is also the fosa, Madagascar's largest carnivore, which is related to the mongoose, and the tiny insectivorous tenrec, which looks like a cross between a shrew and a hedgehog. The rich variety of animal life is matched by an amazing 8500 species of vascular plants, including around 1000 species of orchid. There are 7 species of baobab (upside-down tree), weird fungi, cactus-like euphorbias and the magnificent ravinala (traveller's palm) displaying its luxuriant fan of fronds. Perhaps due to the upsurge in eco-tourism throughout the world, conservation has become a priority in Madagascar. Funds from government and international agencies have been directed to the national parks and nature reserves, and attempts are being made to educate the local population in less destructive farming methods.

In many respects the people of Madagascar must also be classed as unique. They are a gentle and gracious people, bound by centuries-old tradition and a complex code of taboos or 'fady'. To them family and ancestors are very important. From time to time, certain tribes go so far as to remove from their tombs the remains of their dead ancestors. This is the ceremony known as 'famadihana' and it involves feasting and celebration, with the remains being wrapped in a new shroud, paraded around and generally treated as if the deceased were still alive. After bringing the deceased up-to-date on all the village news, the remains are returned to the tomb. It is hoped that by looking after the ancestors in this way, they in turn will look after the living, ensuring good rains, abundant crops and healthy livestock.

II TRAVEL AND YACHT CHARTER INFORMATION

For travel to Madagascar, a passport and visa are required. It is recommended that you obtain a visa in advance. You should be able to get one for a maximum stay of 3 months. Visas can be obtained at ports of entry, but are more expensive and only cover you for a maximum stay of one month. If leaving by air, there is an airport tax.

For up-to-date details, contact :-
The Embassy of The Republic of Madagascar
2374 Massachusetts Avenue, NW,
Washington, DC 20008   Tel. (202) 265 5525/6 E-mail malagasy@embassy.org
The Malagasy Consulate in New York City Tel. (212) 986 9491 or
Your nearest Malagasy Embassy or Consulate.

(National Holiday is Independence Day, 26 June.)

The main ports of entry are Antananarivo (the capital, by air), Antsiranana (Diego Suarez), Antsohimbondrona, Mahajanga (Majunga), Toamasina (Tamatave), and Toliara (Tulear). Yachts may also check in and obtain visas at Andoany (Hellville) when arriving from the north, and at Morombe or Morondava when coming from the south.

Regarding disease prevention, you would be well-advised to obtain vaccinations against cholera, yellow fever and hepatitis, and to take anti-malarial medications, although the authorities do not seem to check vaccination certificates these days.

The following airlines serve Madagascar :-

Air Madagascar

31 avenue de l'Indépendance, BP 437,

101 Antananarivo   Tel. +26120 222 2222 Fax. +26120 222 5728

http://www.air-mad.com

In South Africa Tel. +2711 289 8222 Fax. +2711 289 8072

E-mail madagascar@traveldirections.co.za

Air France

British Airways

KLM Royal Dutch Airlines

Kenya Airways

Delta Airlines

TWA

American Airlines

Details of all airline timetables, fares, etc can be obtained from
Expedia at
http://msn.expedia.com/pub/agent

Official tourist offices to contact are :-
Direction du Tourisme de Madagascar
Ministry of Tourism, BP 610,
101 Antananarivo   Tel. +26120 222 6298 Fax. +26120 222 6710
Maison du Tourisme
place de l'Indépendance, BP 3224,
101 Antananarivo   Tel. +26120 223 2529 Fax. +26120 223 2537
Madagascar Tourist Office
124 Lomas Santa Fe Drive, Suite 206,
Solana Beach, CA 92075   Tel. 1-800-854-1029 (Toll-free in USA)
E-mail info@cortez-usa.com
E-mail in Madagascar cortez-MAD@mcimail.com
Travel agencies and yacht charter companies to contact are :-
Animaltracks and Islandventures at
http://www.animaltracks.co.za/madagascar/index.html
They can arrange skippered charters on catamaran 'Helena I', motor
yacht 'Uthingo' or 45 foot monohull 'Dreamchild'.
    Unusual Destinations at http://www.unusualdestinations.com or
info@unusualdestinations.com or Tel. +2711 706 1991 Fax. +2711
463 1469
    They can arrange skippered charters on 12 metre Dean catamaran
'Bossi' through
    Island Quest Adventures, or contact http://www.islandquest.co.za or
    strauss@dts.mg or Tel. +26120 866 1556 or +2711 706 1991 Fax.
+2711 463 1469.
    Ocean Sailing Academy, 38 Fenton Road, Durban 4001, Rep. of
South Africa.
    Tel. +2731 301 5726 Fax. +2731 3071257

http://www. oceansailing.co.za or academy@oceansailing.co.za

They provide 3-week sail-training vacations to Madagascar.

Madagascar   Discovery   Agency   at   http://www.madagascar-contacts.com

They arrange sailing boat cruises on 'Erol II'

Lions on the Beach—Adventure Travel Video Production

http://home.flash.net/^lions/ or lions@flash.net

They have a sailing yawl, 'Sara', in Madagascar.

Ever Onward Personalized Vacations

http://www.everonward.com/mill.html or linda@everonward.com

They provide yacht charters worldwide, including 'Nosy Pearl' in Madagascar.

A To Sea Yachting Inc.

http://www.atosea.com

They have an 88 foot motor-sailer, 'Katiouchka', in Nosy Be.

Boatz 'n Yachtz Bareboat and Crewed Charters

http://www.boatznyachtz.com

They have monohulls and catamarans in various locations, including the Indian Ocean and Madagascar.

VPM Dufour Yacht Charter

http://www.VPM.fr

They provide a skippered fleet of yachts which migrates (Mar-Nov) from the Seychelles to Madagascar. Charters there are from Nosy Be to the Mitsio Islands and return.

Croisières de Cool Sailing
http://usine.pointfr.com/cool/croisieres/crois.msql
They provide yacht charters to the Mitsio Islands.
South African Marine Industry Buyers' Guide
http://www.steerage.co.za and www.cruiser.co.za
They provide a marine search engine and a forum for cruising people.
Local contacts in Madagascar for accommodation and/or yacht charter:-
Nosy Iranja Islands-Dreams Tel. +26120 866 1690 or 032 070 6830
Madavoile Blue Planet Tel. +26120 866 1637 or +26120 866 1431

Bibliography

I GENERAL BACKGROUND READING

'Dancing With The Dead: A Journey Through Zanzibar and Madagascar' Helena Drysdale, Publ. Hamish Hamilton 1991.

'Guide To The Birds of Madagascar' Olivier Langrand, Publ. Yale University Press 1990.

'Lemurs of Madagascar and The Comoros: The IUCN Red Data Book' Compiled by Caroline Harcourt with assistance from Jane Thornback, Publ. IUCN 1990.

'The Aye-Aye and I: A Rescue Expedition in Madagascar' Gerald Durrell, Publ. Harper Collins 1992.

'Complete Guide to The South Western Indian Ocean: Comores, Madagascar, Mauritius, Reunion, Seychelles' Iain Wallker, Publ. Lascelles 1993.

'Madagascar Wildlife: A Visitor's Guide' Hilary Bradt, Derek Schuurman, Nick Garbutt, Publ. Bradt 1996.

'Spectrum Guide to Madagascar' Publ. Nairobi: Camerapix 1997.

'Madagascar and The Comoros' Paul Greenway and Deanna Swaney, Publ. Lonely Planet 1997.

'Muddling Through in Madagascar' Dervla Murphy, Publ. Flamingo 1998.

'A Visitor's Guide to Madagascar' Marco Turco, Publ. Southern Book Distributors/Struik 1998.

'Madagascar: The Bradt Travel Guide' Hilary Bradt, Publ. Bradt Publications Jan 2000

'Madagascar and The Comoros' James and Deborah Penrith, Publ. Oxford: Vacation Work 2000.

'The Eighth Continent: Life, Death and Discovery in the Lost World of Madagascar' Peter Tyson, Publ. Morrow, William and Co. Jun 2000.

'Africa and Madagascar: Total Eclipse 2001 and 2002' A. Irwin, H. Bradt, S. Williams, Publ. Globe Pequot Press Nov 2000.

Europa World Book entry on Madagascar. Published annually by Europa Publications Ltd.

Encarta entry on Madagascar at http://encarta.msn.com

CIA World Factbook at
http://www.cia.gov/cia/publications/factbook/indexgeo.html

Lonely Planet—Destination Madagascar at
http://www.lonelyplanet.com/destinations/africa/madagascar/

Lonely Planet—Travellers' Reports at
http://www.lonelyplanet.com/letters/afr/mad_pc.htm

Eclipse information at eclipse@eclipsesolaire.com

II PILOT BOOKS AND OTHER PUBLICATIONS, CHARTS AND CHART AGENTS.

'Admiralty Tide Tables Volume 3. Indian Ocean and South China Sea' British Admiralty.

'Indian Ocean South, Pilot and Supplement' British Admiralty, 1995.

'Light List Volume D. Atlantic (East), Western Indian, Arabia' British Admiralty Annual Publication.

'Atlas of Pilot Charts: Indian Ocean' National Imagery and Mapping Agency, 1991.(USA)

'Sailing Directions: East Africa and South Indian Ocean' NIMA, 1995. (USA)

'East Africa Pilot' Delwyn McPhun, Publ. Imray, Lawrie, Norie & Wilson, 1998. Excellent and very readable guide aimed at the cruising yachtsman.

List of British Admiralty Charts:-

Chart No.	Scale	Description
679	50000	Anchorages on E. Coast of Madagascar
680	36000	"　　"　"　"　"　　"
692	64980	Rade de Tulear & Baie de St Augustin
701	150000	Approaches to Baie de Bombetoke
704	145000	Nosi Shaba (Nosy Beroja) to Moramba Bay, incl. Narendri Bay
706	100000	Iles Mitsio to Baie d'Ampasindava
718	100000	Islands N. of Madagascar
758	1000000	N. Apps to Madagascar
760	1000000	Baie d'Ampasilava to Mananjary
1810	1000000	Porto de Bartolomeu Dias to Porto Antonio Enes with W.Coast of Madagascar

2110 Channel	1000000	N. Entrance to Mocambique
2461 Madagascar	100000	Plans on N. & W. Coasts of
2871	25020	Nosi Be Southern Anchorages
3855	350000	Cape Kimby to Morombe
3868	350000	Cape Kimby to Cape St Andre
3871	350000	Baie de Bombetoke to Cap St Andre
3872	350000	Nossi Be to Baie de Bombetoke
3873	350000	Iharana to Nosy Be

List of NIMA Charts:-

Stock No.	Scale	Title
61ACO61300	1000000	Madagascar- N. Coast & Seychelles
61ACO61400 Reaches	1000000	Mozambique Channel- Northern
61ACO61410	300000	Tanjona Bobaomby to Nosy Be
61ACO61420	300000	Nosy Be to Helodrano Bombetoka
	50000	A: Nosy Be Anchorage
61ACO61430 Vilanandro	300000	Helodrano Bombetoka to Tanjona
61ACO61440 Kimby	300000	Tanjona Vilanandro to Tanjona
61ACO61450	1000000	Mozambique Channel
61ACO61460	300000	Tanjona Kimby to Nosy Lava
61ACO61470	300000	Nosy Lava to Toliara (Tulear)
	300000	B: Toliara to Cap Andriamanao
61ACO61500	1000000	Madagascar S. Coast
61ACO61510 Karimboly	300000	Tanjon Andriamanao to Cap des
	300000	B: Cap des Karimboly to Faradofay
(Ft Dauphin)		
61ACO61520	300000	Tolanaro to Ambalavato

	300000	B: Faraony
61ACO61530	300000	Faraony to Mahanoro
	300000	B: Mahanoro to Toamasina
61ACO61540	300000	Toamasina to Tanjon Antsirakosy
61ACO61550	1000000	Madagascar- E. Coast
61ACO61560	300000	Tanjon Antsirakosy to Iharana
	300000	B: Iharana to Tanjona Bobaomby
61BHA61331	100000	Baie Andranoaomby to Helodranon
Antsiranana		
61BHA61433	100000	Apps to Baie de Bombetoka
61BHA61434	25012	Helodrano Bombetoka
61BHA61472	50000	Toliara (Tulear) and Apps
	20000	A: Toliara (Tulear)
61BHA61522	100000	Faradofay (Ft Dauphin) and Apps
	15000	A: Faradofay (Ft Dauphin)
61BHA61538	75000	Toamasina and Apps
	15000	Plan: Toamasina
61BHA61562	30000	Helodranon Antsiranana
	15000	A: Helodranon Antsiranana

Chart Agents and other useful contacts:-

The UK Hydrographic Office http://www.hydro.gov.uk or generalenquiries@ukho.gov.uk

Imray, Lawrie, Norie & Wilson http://www.imray.com or ilnw@imray.com

Sea Books http://www.seabooks.com or armchair@seabooks.com

Navicharts On-Line Chart Catalogue http://www.navicharts.no or jaat@navicharts.no

Maryland Nautical sales@mdnautical.com

NOAA/NIMA Catalog of Hydrographic Products http://www.nima.mil or marine_navigation_contacts@nss.nima.mil

The Tyneside International Admiralty Chart Agents (Durban, South Africa) http://www.tyneside.co.za

Tony Herrick, Cruising Connections, 7 Fenton Lane, Durban 4001, Rep. of South Africa. Excellent place to get reasonably-priced used charts and publications, as well as new ones. Contact Tony at worldsail@mweb.co.za

III LIST OF WAYPOINTS

List of waypoints actually used during the voyage of 'Gone With the Wind' to Madagascar:-

Durban	29° 50' S	31° E
Tulear	23° 30' S	43° 25' E
Tulear Approaches	23° 20' S	43° 35' E
Salary	22° 35' S	43° 14' E
C. St Vincent	22° S	43° 09' E
Morombe	21° 45' S	43° E
C. Ankarana	20° 30' S	43° 51' E
Morondava Apps	20° 18'.3 S	44° 12' E
C. Kimby	18° 55' S	44° 4'.5 E
C. St Andre	16° 19' S	44° 10' E
	16° 04' S	44° 17'.5 E
Majunga	15° 37' S	46° 10' E
	15° 20' S	46° 10' E
Nosy Saba	14° 25' S	47° 35' E
Nosy Iranja	13° 40' S	47° 48' E
Nosy Be	13° 26' S	47° 58'.5 E
Iles Mitsio	13° 04' S	48° 30' E
Iles Glorieuses	11° 40' S	47° 22' E

Useful waypoints N. of Durban, South Africa:-

Boteler Point	27° 01' S	32° 53' E
Jesser Point	27° 33' S	32° 42' E
C. Vidal	28° 08' S	32° 36' E
C. St Lucia	28 ° 32' S	32° 25'.5 E
Nhlabane Rock	28° 40' S	32° 19' E
Richards Bay Light	28° 48' S	32° 10' E
Richards Bay Apps	28° 52' S	32° 05' E
Tugela	29° 14' S	31° 38' E

Printed in Great Britain
by Amazon.co.uk, Ltd.,
Marston Gate.